Alligator
MARINES

A story of the 5th Amphibious
Tractor Battalion in WW II

Saipan   Tinian   Iwo Jima

Donald B. Marshall

ALLIGATOR Marines

Copyright © 2007 by Donald B. Marshall
2nd Printing: February 2010
2nd Edition September 2013
2nd Printing on 2nd Edition November 2015

Published in the United States. All rights reserved. No part of this book may be reproduced in any form or by any means, electronic or mechanical, including photocopying, recoding, or by any information storage and retrieval system, without the written permission of the publisher or author.

Publisher: Day By Day

Author: Donald B. Marshall

ISBN 978-1-934569-20-7 Paperback
ISBN 978-1-934569-21-4 Digital
Library of Congress Control Number: 2013951299

ALLIGATORMARINES.COM

CONTENTS

INTRODUCTION vii

FOREWORD xi

Chapter 1: You are not superman 1

Chapter 2: Murphy's Law . . . Murphy must have been a Marine 9

Chapter 3: When in doubt, empty the magazine 15

Chapter 4: Over the bounding main 19

Chapter 5: A slow race to combat 25

Chapter 6: Don't look conspicuous; it draws fire 29

Chapter 7: How the 5th saved the life of General McArthur 37

Chapter 8: When you have secured an area, don't forget to tell the enemy 49

Chapter 9: Anything you do can get you shot. . . including doing nothing 55

Chapter 10: Important things are simple; It's the simple things that are hard 61

Chapter 11: Make it too tough for the enemy to get in, and you can't get out 65

Chapter 12: Teamwork is essential; . . . it gives them other people to shoot at 71

Chapter 13: How to survive in spite of yourself 75

Chapter 14: You will enjoy recreation, whether you like it or not 81

Chapter 15: Professionals are predictable but the world is full of amateurs 87

Chapter 16: Try to look unimportant; they may be low on ammo 91

Chapter 17: Leaving Paradise 97

Chapter 18: A band of brothers 101

Chapter 19: " . . I am proud and feel honored to fight until death comes . . ." 109

Chapter 20: We have repulsed the enemy 113

Chapter 21: The Marines are coming . 119

Chapter 22: "Four days? This will be like shooting ducks." 123

Chapter 23: Impossible to remember but impossible to forget 127

Chapter 24: This s as bad as it can get, but don't bet on it 135

Chapter 25: The careful application of terror is also a form of communication 141

Chapter 26: There is absolutely no substitute for the lack of preparation 145

Chapter 27: Someone who thinks logically is a nice contrast to the real world 155

Chapter 28: Friends may come and friends may go, but enemies accumulate 163

Chapter 29: By the time you make both ends meet, they move the ends 171

Chapter 30: If it's stupid, but works, it ain't stupid 177

Chapter 31: If you are short of everything except the enemy, you are in combat 183

Chapter 32: All five-second grenade fuses are really three seconds 191

Chapter 33: Leaving the Japanese Alamo 199

Chapter 34: The great adventure ends 201

Epilogue: I BECAME A MARINE 206

A note about the illustrations.

All of these drawings were done by the author generally using Japanese paper with their pens or pencils that he took off dead bodies or sketched on the backs of letters from home. Many were drawn at night by candlelight on board the wrecked ship described in Chapter 29. Others were drawn on ship while returning to Maui after the battle of Iwo Jima. Drawn by a 17 year old amid the ravages of war, they communicate a stark reality of the revulsion of war and the price of freedom. You can see his drawing skills improve as time goes by. Don't look at the illustrations and judge him as a "poor artist." Donald was not trying to be an artist but record what he saw so that he could remember and share when the war ended.

During WWII, political correctness was not in style and as such, my Dad's drawings are unaffected by the current malaise called "political correctness." His story is also unaffected by it and I ask you not to judge him or this book by using the PC filter. I could have edited out the harsher sections and most outrageous words. I chose not to. This story should be read as one who wants to know what *really* happened, how people *really* thought and felt, not life as we would like to remember it. It is real. It is stark. It is World War II on the pacific front.
~Shelly Marshall, daughter of the author.

INTRODUCTION

After a series of crushing American defeats throughout the vast pacific, the United States Marines fought battles at Guadalcanal, Tulagi, Tanagogo and Gavutu, in the first successful land actions against the Empire of Japan.

It was in these steamy islands where Marines adopted new techniques and tools to whip a tough and very clever enemy, tools and methods that would save many American lives in future actions. One of these new tools was the fat, clumsy *LVT*, 'landing vehicle, tracked,' more commonly known as the Alligator.

In 1937, *Life Magazine* ran a story titled "Roebling's Alligator of Florida Rescue." The article centered on a raft-like vehicle being developed by engineer John Roebling and his son Donald for hurricane and/or swamp rescues.

Admiral Edward Kalbfus, recognizing the potential for amphibious operations, brought the article to the attention of General Louis Kittle and other USMC brass. A study was ordered. After a bit of a hassle, the Navy Bureau of Ships floated enough funds to develop this mobile raft. Roebling was not interested in the military aspect of the machine, but, after a bit of persuasion, he agreed to build another. He began working on a new model in 1940 at an estimated price tag of $20,000. It was completed for $16,000. Roebling wanted to return the balance, but his offer caused no end of confusion, as this had never before been done. Eventually, the vehicle was taken to Culebra Island for tests. Though underpowered and with unreliable tracks, it ran reasonably well, enough so that 100 Alligators were ordered.

In the spring of 1941, 26 Second Lieutenants were sent to Dunedin, Florida, under command of Major W. W. Davies, for training on these strange new crawlers. Second Lt. George Shead was one so assigned. When the war started, these officers and a few enlisted men were the only trained tractor men in the service. Realizing the potential of alligator men and their machines, Davies vigorously promoted expansion. Major Davies moved to Fleet Marine Force, Pacific (FMFPAC) as amphibious advisor. First and 2nd Amphibious Tractor battalions were formed as divisional units and so numbered. Alligator Marines, untried but eager, charged in combat with these huge, clumsy machines that were still in the early stages of development. Refinement would come only when the crews gained experience, and that came when the bullets were flying.

The first models, *LVT-1s,* clanked ashore in the South Pacific under many a jaundiced eye, not as assault weapons, but as cargo carriers.

Once in action, these ponderous, ugly monsters totally confused everyone, including the enemy.

Assuming certain terrain impassable to Marines, the Japanese occupying Guadalcanal concentrated their efforts on more defensible positions. They were appalled when the slow, clanking machines, which also served as a mobile machine gun platform and a rough but reliable ambulance, began rumbling through impassable territory with men and materials and, when idle, took up armored guard duty on the perimeter of camps, beaches and the all-important Henderson airfield.

Food Machinery Corp. of Riverside, California, an unlikely facility for building these cumbersome vehicles, was awarded the first contract. Their engineers eagerly awaited modifications recommended by the men in the best position to know . . . the Alligator Marines in the South Pacific.

Soon, improved *LVTs* were taking part in other actions. Halfway around the world, they delivered Army troops and supplies ashore against Vichy French positions in North Africa. Army command moved the *LVTs* north and engaged them in the Aleutians in the summer of 1943, then again at Rendova and Bougainville. Each time, the *LVT* proved itself a reliable and useful cargo vehicle but *had yet to be tested under direct fire* during an amphibious assault. This was soon to change.

Atolls are small, low island chains surrounded by protective coral reefs. As foreseen by those early Marine Corps planners, the *LVT* would be the ideal vehicle to overcome such barriers. Most of the thousands of atolls in the Pacific were fortified and occupied by the Japanese. Their presence caused serious logistical problems to the American war effort.

Makin and Tarawa atolls were the first in line for elimination. Heavily fortified Tarawa with its valuable airfield posed a constant threat to Allied communications. It was to be taken by the 2nd Div. Marines. Makin, 100 miles to the north, would be the Army's responsibility.

Major General Julian C. Smith, Commander of the 2nd Div., pointed out that Tarawa's reef would require more amphtracs than the 100 currently in his 2nd Amph Battalion. Furthermore, the machines available were in sorry shape after Guadalcanal.

Admiral Kelly Turner disagreed, insisting the Navy's usual landing craft, the *LCVP*—'Landing Craft Vehicle, Personnel,' aka Higgins boat, would be satisfactory. Smith exploded and stated flatly that, if *LVTs* were not used, there would be no invasion!

Eventually, 75 of the *LVT-1s* were reconditioned, and an additional 50 of the new *LVT-2s* were located and formed into a new company. Battalion Commander Major Henry Drewes foresightedly ordered makeshift boiler plate armor attached to the fronts of the vehicles to bolster their original quarter-inch skin. The *LVT-1s* were armed with a .50-caliber machine gun forward and a .30 aft. The *LVT-2s* were fitted with .50- and .30-caliber machine guns forward and a single .30 aft. Grappling hooks were also fitted onto the tractors to pull up any barbed wire barriers.

On 20 November 1943, 100 amphtracs in three waves began their slow crawl toward Betio, one of the 47 islands comprising the Tarawa atoll chain. Betio contained the airfield. As predicted, the tractors easily scaled the coral reef, while the following waves of Turner's *LCVPs* became hopelessly stranded. The Navy's pre-invasion bombardment had been less than effective, and all the 42 tracs in the first wave caught heavy enemy fire. Eight were immediately destroyed. Four Alligators plowed through the bombardment and proceeded inland. The attackers sprang over the sides, while the drivers, taking advantage of their newly acquired armor, backed out. Other tractors unloaded on the beach. Those not knocked out returned to the stranded Navy boats again and again to bring in Marines. Fifteen sank due to numerous holes in the hulls, while others suffered killing direct hits. As the tractor numbers diminished, round trips became fewer and fewer. Hundreds of Marines were left in neck-deep water to wade the deadly six to eight hundred yards to the beach.

Eventually, twenty-five more machines were rushed in, and Tarawa was taken, but the Marine cost was high—1056 dead, 2292 wounded, 72 tractors destroyed, and another 20 failed with mechanical problems. Of the remainder, all suffered hits. Yet, the sad experience of Tarawa saved lives later on, for it proved the immense value of the fat, unlovely *LVT*.

Most Marine Corps units have official histories recorded by the Navy Department or by professional historians. Divisions, battalions and regiments have been extolled in movies, by television or by various publications. Not so with the Alligator Marines of the Fifth Amphibious Tractor Battalion . . .

We were always the footnote.

FOREWORD

"Pssst", The sound, coming from a shadowed area between two ancient buildings in the French quarter of a picturesque area of New Orleans, Louisiana, alerted United States Marine Corps Captain Daniel J. Reagan to be on his guard. It was January 1943, and Captain Reagan was stranded, unable to board a train or bus bound for Camp Pendleton, California. He was to join a new unit, the 5th Amphibious Tractor Battalion. Reagan was a Guadalcanal vet of the 1st Amphtrac Battalion and served with Marines such as Stoll, Polack, Pavenski, Small and others who were already "on board" the Fifth Amphs after their leaves at home.

"Pssst," again, followed by a low voice, "Mi Capitan over here, I hear you weesh to purchase, how you say, are in the markeet for automovile. Eef yoou follow pleeze I may be able to help you."

Cautious after months in the steaming jungles of the South Pacific, fighting fanatic Japanese, Captain Reagan did not immediately respond until he assessed the situation, "Who are you and who told you I need a car?"

"Does it matter, weeth what you call 'rationing' such machines are difficult to get." A slouching figure emerged from the gloom of the alley. "Follow me," the low voice ordered. Reagan tried to place the accent; French, Haitian, Creole, no matter, it was true, he did need a car. The orders in his pocket required him to report to Camp Pendleton, California, with all due speed. Traveling in comfort of an automobile certainly surpassed the jolting, smelly, crowded confines of wartime railroad travel. "Sure, I need a car."

A short walk following the mysterious figure brought Reagan to the side door of a sleazy waterfront warehouse. Within the dark recess the captain was able to discern a huge hulk covered with canvas. The canvas was carefully folded off revealing a tan 1933 four door 12 cylinder *Pierce - Arrow* automobile.

Examination showed the vehicle to be in reasonably well kept condition, including the all-important tires. There was only one little problem, no papers and no license plates. The original asking price of eight hundred was immediately brought down to a more reasonable figure. "Three hundred," offered Danny.

"Mi capitan yoou are cutting my heart out, look at the good condition, the upholstery, hardly any mileage. Mi capitan I am bleeding."

"Yeah, so am I. How come no papers or license plates eh?"

"Mi capitan the fool crew aboard that dirty Brazilian rusting bucket of a freighter, are a bunch of ignorant Turks, evidently misplaced them while unloading this fine machine. It was night you know, aah, such important documents. Such a loss, I am bleeding," he paused, "how about five hundred?"

"How about three fifty?"

"It is cutting my heart out but four hundred and you can drive it home."

"Done."

Capt. Reagan was a very resourceful person and the records of the war-time gas rationing board of Lafayette Parish, Louisiana, show that he appeared before that board and requested sufficient gasoline coupons to drive a 1933, 12-cylinder Pierce - Arrow automobile from New Orleans to Camp Pendleton by way of San Diego.

The reason given by Reagan for the trip, was to see a sick and dying mother in San Diego, before reporting to a secret unit being formed to go overseas to fight against the enemies of this great country. With tears in his eyes, he made his plea, notwithstanding the fact that his mother was in good health and living in Philadelphia and the unit was no secret; hell, Tokyo Rose knew who we were, where we were going, and the names of our officers. A few months later she even mentioned how many tractor transmissions Bill Clark and his men had to repair while en route to Saipan.

The rationing board was moved by the sincerity of Captain Reagan and, with tears in their eyes, granted his request.

Reagan received gasoline coupons for 200 gallons of gas based on a distance of 2,000 miles at 10 miles per gallon.

No motor trouble developed along the way, and picking up uniformed hitch-hikers and transporting them to the next city augmented the cost of gasoline (20 cents per gallon).

Captain Reagan reported on time to the Pendleton Boat Basin, ready to assume his duties as an Amph. Trac. Officer.

The Pierce - Arrow was very popular and became a liberty car for officers and some enlisted men each weekend as it made its way to Oceanside, San Diego, or Los Angeles. In spite of rationing, gasoline was no problem. 5th Amphs was a mechanized outfit and had a gasoline dump. Occasionally, in the middle of the night the guard would be relieved by the Captain to get a cup of coffee at the mess hall. Under the back seat of the vehicle were several 5-gallon cans. Not that any gasoline was taken from the dump, but strangely enough the gauge of the old Pierce - Arrow never hit the empty mark.

It was discovered that Captain Reagan and the famous actress Jeanette McDonald were high school friends. Jeanette invited Reagan and three other officers to a posh party at her home in Brentwood.

It was a gala affair with all the fine food and liquor anyone could ask for. The party was a grand success until Ms. McDonald (Mrs. Gene Raymond) discovered the captain and her pedigreed dog sharing drinks. The dog was quite drunk. The Marines were escorted to the door by security.

All good things do come to an end, and soon the 5th was ordered to embark. What to do with the car? There were no papers, remember, but such mundane problems are easily solved by determined Marines. Captain Reagan simply drove south of the border to Tijuana, Mexico, and there found a willing buyer with the unusual Latino name of Juan.

Juan agreed to a price of $400, the original cost. However, he insisted in paying the entire amount in two-dollar bills. It took almost a full hour for Juan to count out the proper amount. Reagan accepted and on his return threw a going away party for all the men. Still, he had plenty of the $2 bills left over. Resourceful Reagan changed them with the men staying stateside, to larger denominations to lessen his burden of packing.

Research into the records of the United States Treasury Department shows that an investigation was held in April and May of 1944 of counterfeit $2 bills being passed in California near Camp Pendleton and from San Diego to Los Angeles. No one was ever charged. By this time the 5th Amphs were aboard ship far out to sea. It seems, however, that Captain Reagan's antics were infectious and were to set the pace for all those attached to the 5th Amphibious Tractor Battalion.

Chapter 1: You are not superman

I lay in that jail cell staring at the stark bulb above the bars, just out of reach. Off to my left, also out of reach, lay the open jail house window. Dark and windy, rain drops skimmed across my brow boosted by the breeze. No more than eight feet one way and six feet the other, the only cell occupant, besides me, was the toilet. My bed consisted of a two foot by six foot iron sheet welded to the wall, supported by two chains. No blanket. No mattress.

By day three, I wondered if it wouldn't have been better to outrun that bull who picked me up in the freight yards of Omaha.

"Take it easy, Mister," my wavering voice implored, "don't shoot." The revolver waving in my face was impressive but this bull didn't look like the hulking railroad cops from the Chicago yards. This one was more like a weasel, small and skinny with a long twitching nose. Maybe I *should* have run. Na, then the weasel would of shot me in the butt.

Never explaining what they booked me for or when I'd get out, the jailer at least let me keep my cigarettes. It gave me a little higher status than the town drunk in one of the four cell blocks. For a sixteen year old, three thousand miles from home, *any* status on a cell block meant something. One of the two guys in the cell across the aisle asked if I had any cigarettes. I did; he poked five pennies through the bars to pay for two. I didn't want the pennies, but they insisted.

"We're getting out tomorrow and joining the Marine Corps. You take the money to get yourself some more smokes. No tell'n *how* long you'll be here."

The next morning they were gone. Later, the jailer handed me a package of little candies called Walnettos. They were from the two guys. Guys I never saw again and never forgot. They didn't just leave me Walnettos, they left me a legacy. The

Marine Corp, they said. I always hoped that they did join the Corp, because they are the reason I promised myself that when I got out of jail, I too would become a Marine

They released me the following day. It took a bit of time, but eventually, I kept my promise.

Marine Recruiting Station on 5th Street in Los Angeles

Battalions formed faster than divisions, and Lt. George Shead soon found himself on a sunny California beach assembling the 5th Amphibious Tractor Battalion. Battle hardened vets of Guadalcanal like Bill "Baldy" Stoll, Lt. Harry Elliot, Sgt. Jack Polack, Cpl. Ted Pavenski, Gunnery Sgt. Sam Small, plus old timers like Danny Reagan, George "Bull" Taylor, armorer, 1st Lts. William Hanzl and Gus Paris, Lt. Mike Zara and Dr. Don Hawkins formed the cadre of the 5th.

The remainder of the battalion consisted of youngsters like me. We were all products of the depression. We came from all states in the Union, from big cities and small farms, from hard working families with no time for vacations. We came from families with an unshakable belief in God, family and country. In those days, a young man's only hope for employment was through the New Deal Agency, the Works Project Administration or the Civil Conservation Corps and, of course, the service. Military enlistees with enough education could qualify for Officer Candidate School. Others, like me, were green, stupid and slated for the ordinary ranks. Regardless, we just couldn't wait to enlist.

I finally got into the Corps through the Marine Recruiting Station on 5th Street in Los Angeles. It was my third try. I had two birth certificates; one put me at 16 and one at 17. I convinced Mom the second one was correct.

Proudly repeating the oath that day, they informed me I was now a Marine. A bus ride down the coast to San Diego with twenty other enlistees did not make us Marines, but, we knew that we were Marines, because, after all, the recruiter had told us so. Furthermore, we all knew that we were tough and could show the Japs a thing or two, as well as the Marine Corps.

Undoubtedly I held an advantage over the others, having ridden freights around the country as a kid. The Corps was my ticket to see the world, fight for glory and get paid, to boot. I vowed to be the greatest.

We arrived at the Marine Corps Recruit Depot, San Diego, California. The grounds were beautiful, as were the California hacienda type buildings. A hint of salt in the air prodded us to breath deep and appreciate our new standing. How nice, I thought. Sixty-two other boots just like me gawked and thought likewise. They, too, had been told that they were Marines.

Our reveries were cut short by vicious barked orders to dispense with our chewing gum, all of our toiletries, including razors, and all reading material. Then, encouraged by some more barking, we double-timed in a stumbling mass to a place where we got rid of the hair on our heads. We then double-timed toward some chicken huts way out in the "boonies."

Boot camp for Platoon 884, 1943

We were numbered Platoon 884, 1943. For the next six weeks, we remained isolated from all known forms of humanity. We were pumped daily full of *esprit de corps,* along with gallons of hypodermics for every conceivable disease known to man. Our spirits soared, while our arms hung, aching and lifeless, at our sides. Our clothing, forevermore known as dungarees, fitted to the closest possible sizes . . . too big and too small.

A galvanized bucket and a scrub brush came with the clothing issue. We were informed that this was our portable laundry. We also received a pith helmet along with our dungarees. The stenciled Globe and Anchor on the left breast of our jacket assured us that we were truly Marines. The only way that we were addressed, however, was "boot," "shitbird," or "stupid."

Everywhere we went was on the double. It was lights out at ten, though we were dead asleep before that. Reveille sounded at 4:45. A faint click on the loudspeaker preceded the bugle call. If I awoke to that click, I had an advantage over the two minutes allowed to dress and stand at attention in the company street.

"I wanna see sixty-two little piles of shit frozen solid to the deck by the time that bugle stops. Do you understand?

"And when I say eyes right, I want to hear those eyeballs click. Do you understand?

"And when I say jump, you don't ask 'why?' you ask 'how high?' Do you understand?"

These words screamed from beneath a campaign hat where stood the meanest individual in the world, a Marine drill instructor, the dreaded D.I.

It had a ramrod for a spine and it had leather lungs and, until we got out of boot camp, it was . . . God.

"Do you understand?" it screamed.

"Yup."

"Sure do, Sarge."

"You bet."

"Whatever you say, boss."

Each of us looked around. We nodded. No doubt about it; we were all in agreement.

"Well, then acknowledge it, goddammit!" the voice screamed. "From now on you say 'Aye, Sir" and say it so's I can hear you."

We said, "Aye, Sir."

"I can't hear you."

"Aye, Sir!"

"I still can't hear you."

In our innocence, we assumed this poor man had a hearing problem. It took five more tries before he heard us.

"AYE, SIR!"

This newly acquired lingo made us feel as though we were really part of the Corps. There were other words to learn. In fact, there was an entire new language. Pogey bait was candy, skivvies were undershorts, Mac was any Marine. But to the Navy (swabbies), we were bellhops, and to the Army (dogfaces), we were jarheads. A mop was a swab and the floor was now a deck. Slopchute was a bar or beer garden. Scoop or scuttlebutt was any news, true or not. The list was extensive, but since it was the only language spoken, we learned it rapidly.

The reward for our vocalization that first day was a short two-mile, double-time trot out to the boondocks, led by Sgt. Allred.

Sgt. Allred never puffed; he never even breathed hard. Though short for a Marine, Allred could dress in a gunnysack and still look sharp. His name was aptly applied because whenever he got mad, which was always, he turned all red. He could jump straight into the air and beat the top of my pith helmet with his swagger stick at least half a dozen times before touching the ground. He considered me the dumbest of the dumb, but he considered other boots in the same light. We were constantly reminded that we were all equally stupid. Because we were so good with our, "Aye, Sir," most mornings he would favor us with a three-mile jog. What exercises he couldn't think up, his sidekick, Sgt. Trook, did.

I hated jogging; I hated sports of any kind. I steered clear of sports in school, and boot camp was no different. Always eager to gain the advantage, I noticed Allred or Trook always led us on our morning jogs past two shadowy buildings. I could drop out without being missed, crouch in the shadows and smoke a cigarette. When the platoon double-timed back, I would fall in and huff with the rest. My absence was never noticed ... I dread to think of the consequences had it been.

Constant instruction filled every minute of every day: how to walk, how to talk and salute, how to close order drill and how to field strip everything from rifles to anvils. At night, everything we had learned that day was repeated over again and again. We watched training films daily, but the only one I remember was an award winning docudrama on how not to catch the clap.

Graduation Day

Graduation day was a day never to be forgotten. Our D.I.s assured us that if we screwed up we would be boiled alive, beheaded and burned at the stake, at which point our troubles would really begin. We marched to the grinder and stood at attention in full combat gear, with everything we owned on our backs. With stirring martial music in the air, we stepped out and marched past the flag-studded reviewing stand. On the command of, "Eyes right!," not one of us stumbled into the other. Boy, were we proud! We marched some more, then halted at attention awaiting the words that would officially recognize us as Marines.

Several stern looking officers glowered down on us. One stepped to the podium and, after a long dissertation on mother, apple pie and patriotism, told us that we were now. . *Marines*! It was the proudest day of my life.

The rest of the officers merely rolled their eyes.

After this impressive ceremony we scrambled aboard 6-x-6 trucks, standing room only. As we pulled out of the gate, we watched Sgt. Allred, with a fierce gleam in his eye, striding determinedly toward a Greyhound bus loaded with new arrivals.

We gratefully departed "Dago" boot camp for our new home at Pendleton. Apparently, the civilians along the route hadn't heard: we were now Marines. We waved and cheered, but they didn't. They just went on with their wartime business. We didn't mind, we were the Few, the Proud, the Marines . . . almost.

Camp Pendleton was beautiful and different. Expecting typical wartime barracks, we were amazed at the Spanish architecture, the gentle rolling hills, and the small lake. Boy, this was the life!

Once again, our pleasant thoughts were brought to a sudden halt. We were again informed that we were not yet Marines, not even close. There was the little matter of the Camp Matthews rifle range. First and foremost, a Marine is a rifleman. We were about to learn the tools of our trade. We soon found those gentle rolling hills to be not so gentle when double-timing at high port to the range every morning. Those trips were uphill both ways. At the range, we flopped on our bellies and wrapped ourselves in a leather strait jacket known as a rifle sling, and then assumed every impossible bone and muscle position known to man.

Standing, kneeling, sitting or lying flat, we fired at a little black dot miles away, in a target area known as the "butts" . . . none of us dared tempt fate with too many maggies drawers (misses). All the while we were firing, a big footed instructor kicked, or slammed, our M-1 or '0-3 rifle barrel, testing proper adjustment of the leather sling. If wrapped in error or too loose, the experience proved quite a jawbreaker.

We cleaned our rifles daily in hot, soapy water and pure fish oil. The rank smell of the oil on our person and clothing did not endear us to Camp Pendleton personnel. This place made us almost homesick for good old boot camp. After a few weeks of target practice, it was time to qualify for score. Expert had $5 added to his pay; sharpshooter got $3. I made sharpshooter.

Then, the big day arrived: assignments. The 1st Sgt. read off names. Some went to fleet Marines or communications, some to cook and baker school, a few to mechanics or rifle companies, and the rest of us were told that, because of our outstanding performance in all aspects of training, we were expendable. We were posted to Alligator school with the newly forming 5th Amphibious Tractor Battalion.

"Expendable! Hey, guys, you hear that? We're expendable! How about that ... uh ... what's expendable mean?"

"Expendable, it means they *expect* to *spend* more money on us than anybody else, dummy."

"I think," the sergeant drolled, jerking a thumb over his shoulder, "You'll find the 5th amphtracs over that way someplace, near the ocean."

[*Graduation Day*]

Chapter 2: Murphy's Law . . . Murphy must have been a Marine

"Near the ocean," meant the boat basin, a vast, windy, dry grass wasteland incised by numerous ravines and canyons. It lay across the highway from Camp Pendleton. A rock-circled hole in the beach formed a small pond, hence the name "boat basin."

We double-timed to our new home only to find it wasn't built yet. There was one mess hall and one headquarters building. Our pyramidal tents, in bundles, were being dumped off a truck. After erecting them, we could move in.

Upon enlisting in the Corps, one forfeits the right to a momma and a poppa. The Corps takes the place of both.

Somehow, the Corps' infinite wisdom allowed it to put together the most compatible, loyal, stick-together bunch ever assembled, the *Alligator Marines*. Of course, every Marine unit says the same thing. Nevertheless, the camaraderie of the Alligator men, officers and enlisted, was to prove itself time and time again. Alligator men were as imperturbable as Private Anthony, USMC, when, in 1898 a terrific explosion rocked the battleship Maine at Havana, Cuba, the private knocked on Capt. Charles Sigsbee's cabin door and matter-of-factly uttered the historic words, "I have to report, Captain, that the ship is sinking."

This became our attitude. Except for those few who slugged it out in the Pacific islands, amphtrac men had no predecessors, no history, and no tradition. Tracked amphibious landing machines were a new baby, less than two years old. We felt right at home.

Marine Corps chow was much better than what I ate while riding freights and far better than what Mom cooked at home. My 180 pounds quickly leapt to 200 pounds. At 6'4", I needed it. Not to be harsh, but my mother competed for the title of worst cook in the world. At home we ate a lot of horse meat,

Alligator Marines

which I liked, but she excelled in cold oatmeal smothered in lard; everything else she screwed up. Here at the boat basin, I tasted Spam for the first time. Oysters, too. I liked both.

New people arrived daily, swelling our ranks to about 500 men. Our schooling began as soon as the tents were up. We had one *LVT-1* and some used *LVT-2s* for a total of eight training vehicles. We started with the 2s, learning everything from mechanics, to floating gunnery, to driving. We found that the tractor speed in water was four to five miles per hour. We soon changed the designation of *LVT, landing vehicle, tracked*, to that of *large vulnerable target.* Slow as they were, they could get out of hand. Second Armored Amphs, who called themselves "Turtles" and were training alongside us, had one of their vehicles escape. It groused through a couple of tents before grinding over another parked machine. Regardless, the low profile of the Alligator in the water was an asset for moving men and material ashore.

The cab of an *LVT* was little more than an iron cocoon. Two brake steering levers for left and right tracks sat on each side of the driver. A clutch pedal occupied the left foot and a gas pedal the right. Cruising a calm sea was easy, but, when heading for a beach or reef, a driver had to be alert and instantly determine the speed and height of a building wave to maintain proper control of the 13 to 15 ton monster. The beach at the boat basin, now Camp Del Mar, boasted some real tricky surf. When approaching the shore, speed of the tracks was all-important. One should not go too fast, and not too slow. The driver had to feel the movement of the waves and try to surf the machine while still keeping directional control. At this critical moment he had to shove in the clutch pedal, release both brake levers and use two hands plus a lot of muscle to ram the gear shift lever into one of the five different speeds. If he were lucky, he might hear the orders shouted by the white knuckled, frantic instructor above, but usually the roar of the transmission and the impact of tons of water through the leaky hatches canceled all communication.

Extra high sneaker waves were very dangerous and impossible to detect. They could force the nose of a tractor into the sand and flip it end over end or pile over the stern and flush a man out of the open cargo compartment. I lost a good friend this way, Zane Grey of Streeter, Illinois. His body washed up a few days later.

Liberty was limited to 24 and 48 hours. Because we were going over soon, we got no furloughs and no 72s. Nearby Oceanside was great; the civilians were always nice. We often snuck in and out of camp via a wooden railroad trestle to the south, over a ravine. I got drunk on one of these escapades and ended up in Apache Jack's tattoo parlor for my first and only tattoo. It was the stupidest three dollars I ever spent.

Paratrooper and Raider Training

Without explanation (such niceties were unnecessary in the Corps) I was sent back to Pendleton to a Casual company that was anything but casual. I joined a platoon going through a Paratroop and Raider physical combat school. A Col. Hanley headed it. He and three sergeants made us wish we were back in boot camp. We double-timed every place, and this was only a small part of our daily routine of navigating inflated boats in the pouring rain at night through a muddy swamp, crawling under machine gun fire, setting booby traps, jujitsu and knife and club combat. In addition we practiced bayonet fighting using 1903 rifles. The eighteen inch bayonets, no scabbards, just bare blades made one move with a great deal of agility. We paired off, instructed in *Biddle* style movements of slice, slice thrust rather than the old style of one step, two step, lunge, thrust. I thought *Biddle a* much better system, and if you weren't fast enough and got cut, it was your fault, not your opponent. Strangely enough, I looked forward to encountering an enemy with whom I'd be able to test my newly acquired talents.

We also made jumps from a fifty-foot tower into an Olympic-sized swimming pool. No matter how large it was at ground level, it shrunk to the size of a postage stamp from that height. I was hesitant my first time up, which I knew would be my last, because I was certain I would miss the pool and splat upon the concrete apron. I was rudely launched with a good swift kick in the butt. As if that weren't enough, we then swam through burning gas, after which we ran some more. This time, there was no way to duck it.

Broomstick whacking on a metal trashcan in the middle of the night signaled the beginning of a ten-mile, full-combat pack and rifle hike. We had to complete the ten miles in one hour and 15 minutes. There was a Marine from 2nd Armored, a sergeant I think, named Mackey, about 30 years old and hard as a rock, who reminded me of Sgt. Allred because he never puffed. If that old man could do it, so could I. On one occasion we did twenty miles. It wasn't long before my pack was crammed with small empty cardboard boxes, skivvies tucked around to smooth out the corners. It saved a lot of weight that way. No one caught me.

A game was devised wherein a sea bag was filled with sand; a ship's cargo net was then wrapped around that and secured with a heavy manila line. The result was a five- to six-hundred-pound sausage-like bulk about six feet long and three feet in diameter. At the blast of a whistle, each thirty-man team tried to muscle the heavy mass across the opposing team's goal line. There was no such thing as a foul. The "game" lasted thirty minutes. I don't think a score was ever made.

For another bit of recreation, the entire platoon donned boxing gloves. We formed a large circle, arms extended forward with all gloves touching. When the whistle blasted (our instructors loved blasting whistles), each contestant swung as hard as he could at the man nearest him. Each round lasted five minutes. I don't ever remember even one man left standing at the end of a round.

"Hey, Sarge, what you trying to do, teach us to be Raiders?"

"No, stupid, we're teaching you to train Raiders."

True or not, I was flattered and looked forward to this particular assignment. Marine Raiders were the toughest fighters around.

Gaining an advantage over an opponent was already second nature to me

Infiltration was easy for me, due partly to dodging railroad bulls when I hopped freights across America. Using the term "bull," a tough, Depression era name for rail police, as well as growing up in Al Capone's town of Cicero, Illinois, made me feel a lot tougher. Such terminology made the other kids feel the same way.

The gang in my neighborhood came from every imaginable ethnic background. We had "Dagos," "Jews," "Mics," "Hienies," and "Bohunks." Sometimes we dropped the usual disparages and called each other "Wops," "Hebes," "Shanties," "Polocks," or "Huns." An African-American was always "Blackie." I was Belgian, a real minority. That posed a problem, so "Hienie," "Dutchman," or sometimes a "Hun" classified me. It was fun and we all got along. I had to learn the rudiments of about six different languages just to survive.

One of our duties as kids was to periodically cross over to the railroad yard, throw rocks at the passing engines and at the same time call the crewmen nasty names.

"You little bastards, we get you, we break your heads, ..." the engineer would yell, while the fireman would deliver each quaint remark with well-aimed chunks of coal. Our injuries were usually minor. We divided the coal equally, except for the kid who had a bruise or a bloody ear; we gave him an extra piece. We then triumphantly carried our booty home for cooking or warmth.

Attending the Marines Raider School reminded me of my first day in the old brownstone elementary school. At the ripe old age of five, I had my first bona fide fight. My mother made me wear knickers and a French beret. As I climbed the stone entry steps, hoots of derision greeted me because of that stupid beret. One kid, bolder and larger than the rest, ran down and yanked it off my head. As much as I hated the damn thing, no one, *absolutely no one*, was going to take it without my permission. Much to the surprise of us both, my fist smacked him on the nose, not once, but twice. He tumbled down the stairs and ran off crying. It seemed a perfect way to begin my school career. From then on, I strutted around at will. They held me in awe; I had whipped a *second grader.*

Fortunately, at the time I enlisted, the beret was not yet part and parcel of the Special Forces uniform. Not to belittle the fighting abilities of the Green Berets, but I may have had problems with such apparel.

In the year 1937 my rough and tumble Ciciero childhood was swapped for the wild, wild west. We exited the past life via a typical depression mode of travel, an old Ford, complete with mattress tied on top and cardboard boxes on the running boards. Dear old Dad was escaping the law or something, because our family name was quietly changed from Michels to Marshall. Six weeks later we arrived in California.

This explains how all the sneaky ways for gaining an advantage over an opponent were already second nature to me. I had the makings of a top-notch Marine.

Chapter 3: When in doubt, empty the magazine

Raider training was great; this was adventure . . . and I got paid fifty bucks a month, less $6.40 for the National Service Life Insurance premium. Still, it was more money than I ever saw in my life. When I made PFC, I got four dollars more plus three for sharpshooter.

We learned that Jap grenades must be struck against a hard surface to arm. They pop like a child's cap pistol. When you hear the pop, run toward the sound, not away. Theoretically, the enemy will throw the grenade over you, and immediately crouch to avoid the blast. He will not see you coming. On the other hand, if he intends to commit suicide, running toward him is not a good idea. The matter was left to one's discretion.

The trainers told us never to use proper names in combat; the Japs used this ploy to entice a man to raise his head. If he does, he is dead. But, hell, I learned that, as a kid, if you were dumb enough to stick your head up, you'd get a rock between the eyes.

The combat course was easy. Accompanied by a coach, we sneaked through a simulated jungle. At unexpected moments a painted plywood figure popped up. Usually a menacing Japanese soldier, it sometimes was another Marine or even a civilian. To shoot or not, that was the problem. My score was perfect when a Jap target popped up. I fired my M-1 from the hip. The shot severed the pole holding the figure. It fell flat. I pumped three more rounds into it.

Ted Williams, my coach and an avid baseball player, asked why I kept shooting after I had blasted it down.

"I wanted to make sure the son-of-a-bitch was dead, Sir."

His only comment, "You'll make a Marine yet, kid."

Another good trick, when on possum patrol checking dead bodies, is to shoot or bayonet every Jap corpse you see. "If it don't stink, stick it!" I violated that rule once, and it almost cost me my life.

Men who had learned the hard way taught us our lessons. We heard how Lt. Col. Frank Goettage and his men were misled into believing that a group of starving Japanese were waiting to surrender at the mouth of the Matanikau River in the Solomons. The colonel and 25 men walked into an ambush. Several men were shot dead immediately. It was a short, fierce fight. With the exception of three who escaped into the surf, all were beheaded. We also heard that Sgt. Major Jacob Vousa, a retired Guadalcanal native police officer, was tied to a tree and questioned by the Japanese regarding Marine forces. After seven sword and bayonet thrusts, Vousa was left for dead. He chewed his way through his bonds and crawled to Marine lines. In spite of a slashed throat, he gasped out the locations and strength of the Japanese positions. The sergeant recovered and was awarded the Silver Star by General Vandergrift. After the war, Queen Elizabeth knighted Vousa.

We hadn't heard of all the atrocities

We hadn't heard, of course, about the beheading of nine Marines captured on Makin Island after Carlson's raid. That bit of news was released after the war, but word trickled down of the massacre of over 400 prisoners of the 91st Philippine Army Division. They surrendered at Bataan; the Japs tied their hands behind their backs with telephone wire, each man looped to the next. Officers and non-coms, in columns four abreast, were marched to the east road by the Pantingan River, where they were systematically beheaded or bayoneted. Sweating executioners were relieved periodically by other Japanese awaiting their turn to participate. The job took over two hours.

Major Pedro L. Felix received four bayonet thrusts to his shoulder and chest, then one through his back. Bodies of others fell atop him, and he was left for dead. He and another soldier survived. Philippine farmers nursed them back to health. These horror stories steeled each of us to ruthlessly cut down the enemy. I made up my mind that this is the way it would be. As a kid in Cicero, I wanted to work for my hero "Big Al" Capone and carry a tommy gun ... to give no quarter and to expect none.

Then the Raider's training was discontinued, but I had already proved myself worthy. Now I almost felt like a Marine. With dress blues, a uniform I wanted badly, being a "real" Marine would have seemed closer. All us Raiders had were our greens, the best clothes many of us ever owned. Still, they looked pretty good on liberty, even if they weren't dress blues to impress the BAMs.

BAM was an acronym for Beautiful American Marine; female Marines, girls who I thought were extremely lovely. They smelled nice. They were soft. Of course, there were certain jarheads that insisted BAM stood for Broad Ass Marine. The girls retaliated by calling us HAMs or RAMs. Hairy Ass Marines or Raggedy Ass Marines. I was too young to qualify for the first, but, after Iwo Jima, I did fall into the second category.

Upon completion of the Raider course, I returned to the boat basin. This time I rode in a jeep. I figured that maybe now I was a Marine. Well, almost.

Chapter 4: Over the bounding main

The original plan for the 5th Amphs called for three months of training in the United States. However, the eight tractors we had at the boat basin, divided among 500 men in the short time allotted, meant a total of three hours of hands-on training for each man. Oh, well, we'll make it up in Hawaii and then, off to combat. Just think, Hawaii for three more wonderful, luau filled months, getting acquainted with the beautiful island Wahines and with the new model *LVT-4s*.

Our battalion and the 2nd Armored Amphs embarked at San Diego in April, 1944, aboard the *S.S. Comet,* the *S.S. William Peffer* and several Landing Ship, Tank, *LSTs*. My C company was aboard the *Comet,* a Liberty ship right off the stocks. New ship, new crew, new passengers, and everyone was seasick. Below deck and around the galley the stench was unbearable. Puke on everything. The captain ordered below decks flushed with high pressure hoses, a great idea. Water was sprayed in by the thousands of gallons. We discovered, only *after* everything was afloat with sloshing stomach contents, that there was no way to pump the water out. The shipyard people had neglected to connect the pumps! A bucket brigade extending from the lower decks, up the gangways and across the weather deck, made things even worse. Sick Marines and sailors slipped, slopped and dropped slimy buckets all over the ship. The vessel was renamed the *S.S. Vomit*. We stunk up the entire Oahu harbor. Several of us dove off the fantail just to lose the stench.

We were quickly shuffled to the Transit Center west of Honolulu. If they hadn't sunk the *Comet,* they should have burned it. A few days later a little peanut whistle, choo-choo train took us to Oahu for our first liberty.

The red light district

Hotel and Water streets were considered the red light districts. Plain black printing on white signs like "Westward Ho," "Pacific," and "Islander" adorned certain buildings, giving no hint as to the delights inside. We stood in line along the sidewalk. There was no buddy buddy cutting in. Upon entering, one forked over three bucks, the standard price, regulated, I think, by the OPA. A small white towel was your receipt until a hostess became available.

The towel bunched and balled between my fidgety fingers. Not afraid, not afraid, I thought. The Marine Corps has a way of making one afraid to be afraid. I couldn't tell my buddies this was my first time.

There was a delay and the Madam barked orders. "Edna," she screamed, "get your ass over here!"

That shocked me; I had never heard anyone speak to a lady in such a manner, at least not around my family. Edna came running. She apologized, smiled sweetly, clasped my hand and led me to a small room.

It proved an enlightening experience.

Charging imaginary foes

The battalion geared up for a landing on some unknown island when I, and eight others, received orders to take packs and rifles and board a small, wooden, inter-island steamer named Pau. No explanation, just go.

We steamed out of Pearl and traveled the night amongst crated chickens and squealing pigs. I recalled the movie "Rain" and honestly expected to meet Sadie Thompson. I slept on deck. In the morning, we arrived at Kahului, Maui. A waiting truck took us so far back into the hills that we thought Sunday wouldn't arrive until the following Thursday. Here, we joined another group of Marines who were as much in the dark as we were.

For the next ten days, mostly in the rain and at night, we charged imaginary foes up and down Maui's extremely high mountains and deep canyons. We would toss each other ropes, dangle and slide off the cliffs, get a compass bearing, then claw our way to the top of some peak only to reverse the procedure down the other side. We were wet, muddy, and tired all the time. There was a major, whom we assumed was absolutely *crazy,* in charge of these antics. Just when we thought we were alone and could sit to enjoy a cigarette, he would pop out of the brush, cursing a blue streak.

"If I can catch you, then the god damned Japs can, too, and they'll cut off your god damned heads!"

He expressed his dissatisfaction by firing a .45 pistol into the air or into the ground at our feet. His name escapes me, and we never figured how he so easily appeared in places that were nearly inaccessible to us.

At this same time and unknown to us, HQ, "A" and "B" companies of our 5th Amph Btn, 2nd Armored Amph Btn, plus the 2nd and 4th Marine Divisions, were practicing assault maneuvers in Malaea Bay somewhere in the blue sea below us. They were preparing for the invasion of Saipan.

Getting used to the "no explanation" thing, we were not surprised when nine of us were trucked to an airfield for my first ride in an airplane. It was a noisy, windy, inhospitable but sturdy DC-3, aka C-47. We flew back to Pearl Harbor and immediately stood guard duty over a bunch of smoking, wrecked *LSTs* that had exploded a few days before. Thirty-four ships nested in the West Lock of Pearl Harbor were part of the fleet operation for Forager, code name for operation Saipan.

Many things had gone wrong

The maneuvers at Malaea had been completed, and many things had gone wrong. On the night of May 14-15, several of the *LSTs* encountered bad weather. Members of the 8th

Marines, 2nd Div., were sleeping topside in an *LCT (Landing Craft, Tank)* fastened to the deck of *LST 485*. The mother ship rolled in heavy seas; The *LCT* slid off the deck and was rammed and sunk by a following ship. Nineteen men went down; five were injured. *LSTs 71* and *390* also lost their deck loads of *LCTs*. Of the three *LCTs* involved, two sank; one was salvaged. The *LCTs* had been designated as mortar batteries and equipped as such.

The rehearsal revealed shortcomings of the plan, and suitable revisions were to be made. The loss of the two smaller ships was caused by excess weight of the mortars and ammunition. As there were no more 4.2-inch mortars, the remaining *LCT* was to be deleted from the battle plans. The surplus 4.2-inch mortar rounds were to be unloaded at the West Loch ammo depot.

Because there were only six regular ammunition ships in the area, 16 of the *LSTs* were designated as ammo carriers for the invasion. They were to carry 750 rounds of 5-inch .38-caliber ammunition each. Ten others were to carry 270 4.5-inch rockets, 6,000 rounds of 40mm and 15,000 rounds of 20mm each. In addition, they all carried 50 to 100 fifty-gallon drums of gasoline for our gas guzzling tractors.

It was a stroke of luck that, except for the usual work parties, many of the crew and the Marines were in town for the weekend. As the ammo was being moved, some fumble fingers goofed or, as some thought, a civilian welding crew sprinkled sparks atop the gasoline drums. No one knew, or ever will know, what caused the first explosion, but the ships, moored close abreast to one another in rows called tares, never had a chance. *LST 353* went up with a roar. After the first explosion, *179* caught fire and blew. Then *39* and *43* exploded, soon followed by *LSTs 69* and *480*. Parts of ships, cargo and bodies went skyward to rain down on nearby ships, the water and the island.

Heroic Army, Navy, Coast Guard and Marine personnel ashore raced in and manned rescue vessels, but many of these men too were lost victims of tons of debris dropping from the sky. The final tally was 163 lives lost, 396 wounded. Mountains of ammo and other vital materials were destroyed. Although the 5th lost only one man, most of our spare tractor parts now lay on the bottom of the Loch. *Operation Forager*,[1] much to the credit of the planners, was reorganized immediately and, with the exception of those left behind, sailed and invaded Saipan on schedule. So here we were, after all that mountain training, left sitting on our butts, watching a bunch of smoldering junk while our 5th Amph buddies went into action. Forager was a big operation, but I didn't know how big. Five hundred thirty-five ships and 127,000 men, and now my chances to get into the action were gone. Shit.

---

[1]

Many years later I learned the reason for our grueling mountain training. Admiral Richard K. Turner included in the original Forager plan a scheme of putting a company of Raiders ashore at night, D minus 1, on the east side of Saipan and Magiciene Bay. We were to infiltrate inland, take possession of the top of Mt. Tapotchau, establish an observation post, then direct artillery and incoming tractors. But aerial recon discovered that our landing site was heavily fortified; any attempt to take it with a small force would be impossible, and the element of surprise would be lost. Our part of the invasion was canceled.

Alligator Marines

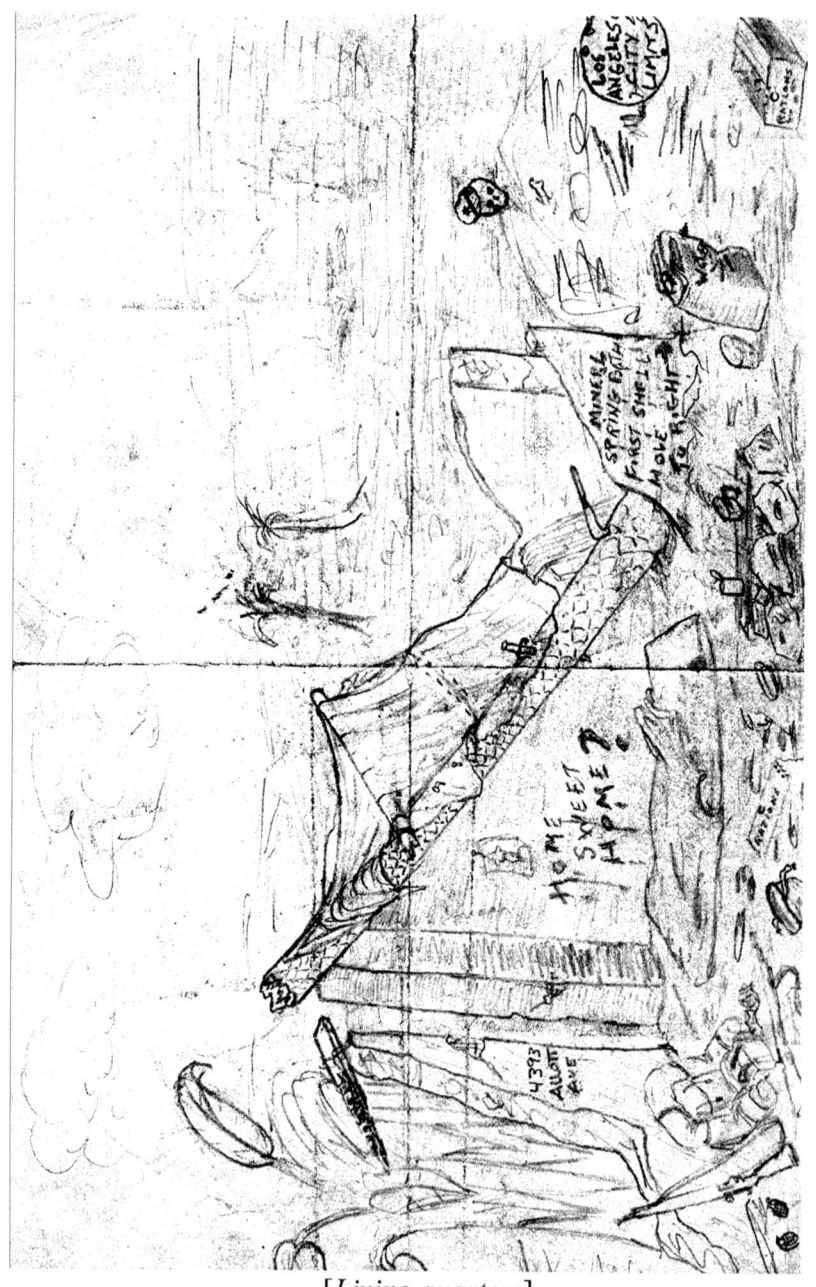

[*Living quarters*]

Chapter 5: A slow race to combat

The *Sea Witch,* a Liberty ship, trailed days behind the invasion fleet. We were supposed to catch up but never did. The ship was slow, eight to ten knots, and always hot, too hot to go below. I swung a hammock (shelter half) from a forward loading boom. No one complained so I spent the next 20 nights under the bright moon, the Southern Cross and a lot of tropical rain.

Life aboard the *Sea Witch* was dull at best except for the usual poker games.

The skipper, who liked to conserve water, prohibited all washing of clothes. While prowling one night, my buddy Eagan and I discovered a flag locker. It contained, in addition to signal flags, a number *of* long lines. These lines would be useful somehow and, after a bit of experimenting, we threaded the rope through the sleeve of a dungaree jacket, one leg of the skivvies and a pant leg, then dropped the clothing off the fantail into the turbulence of the wake. The system did an excellent job of washing. At first, we were going to charge rent for the use of the lines but then shared them for free. The washing had to be done at night.

In addition to being chintzy on water, the captain demanded a tight ship. He nearly laid a brick when he discovered a dozen or more bundles of laundry trailing his ship as it plowed through enemy waters.

He screamed for a Bo's'n with a sharp knife to ". . . cut every damned line and let the clothes drift. By God, those Marines will learn a thing or two about Navy discipline!"

"But, Sir," the Bo's'n began, "the signal officer says ..."

"I don't care what the signal officer says; cut those damned lines!"

The order was promptly carried out.

"That's better, by God. Now . . . what was it you were saying about the signal officer?"

"Uh ... he said all the lines for the signal flags are missing."

Our water ration was cut to one canteen a day.

Salt-water showers were the only way to cool off aboard this bucket of rivets. It was impossible to use regular soap, so we were issued salt water soap; a brown solidified goo that left a residue of tar on the skin.

Those of us who stayed on deck kept a sharp eye for rain squalls. When we spotted one moving our way, we stripped naked and grabbed a bar of real soap. The ship sailed through the deluge for only two or three minutes before momentum carried it from under this blessing. Time allowed only a quick soaping and immediate rinse, but it was worth it.

We always encouraged those less fortunate who chose to remain below amid the foul odors and sweat to come up and enjoy the fresh water provided by Mother Nature. We did not tell them of the urgency of an immediate rinse.

Our victims would leisurely soap themselves with thick sudsy lather from head to foot before noticing the squall had passed, and the hot tropical sun was rapidly encasing them in a cocoon of dried soap impossible to get off until the next squall. The scene was always good for a belly laugh.

The real knee slapper, though, was the ship's head . . . a U-shaped trough about twenty feet long, eighteen inches across, equipped with short movable boards that adjusted to the size of one's butt. Seawater constantly flowed through the trough. At any given time, there were about ten men sitting in a row.

There were two parts to this trick. The first, divert the sitters' attention with a serious conversation that could interest the group without too much effort. The theory of relativity, for instance. Most everyone agreed they didn't give a damn for relatives. That would keep them going for a while. The price of beer was a good subject. Ten cents was too much. It was preferable to steal it whenever possible, never from another Marine though. These subjects really mattered, and sometimes very hot discussions ensued, which suited our purposes exactly, while a cohort smuggled in a large wad of paper, ignited it while he innocently sat down at the inflow end of the trough and dropped it atop the flowing water. The second sitter in line would only feel the warmth of a small flame as the burning paper gathered strength and speed on its journey. By sitter number five, the flame grew to about ten inches. From there on, the victims jumped straight into the air, cursing a blue streak while wildly fanning their smoking behinds. The girls back at Pendleton would be delighted to use the acronym of BAMs on these guys, Bald Ass Marines. The last part of the trick dictated a very quick exit.

Of course, we usually targeted swabbies because they were dumber.

The plot by the ship's captain

Finally, someone designated a day of reckoning. The ship's loudspeaker announced a special treat for all Marines. Speculation ran high. Ice cream? Possibly a special movie? Something besides John Wayne in "Stagecoach," winning the West, or John Wayne winning the war as a Sea Bee, a pilot, a sub commander or a Marine. We were sure tired of that stuff. Almost anything else was welcome.

We waited; the suspense was terrible.

Then, the ship's speaker blared, "Now hear this, now hear this! All Marines will remove all clothing except for combat boots and steel helmets. Marines will then assemble on the fantail at #1 medical station for shots and short-arms inspection."

Short arms referred to one's private parts. We assembled, as ordered, amid much protesting . . . whose silly idea was this?

Our names were called; we clomped to the assigned station, we stood at attention, if one can stand at attention wearing only boondockers and helmets, we recited rank and serial number. There were five stations, each consisting of a table with seated, grinning, corpsman and or doctor. Between these stations spanning the entire length of the ship, lounged a crowd of those stupid, uncaring, knee-slapping, hooting dumb sailors laughing and cat-calling crude remarks about various parts of our delicate anatomy. Obviously this was a plot by the ship's captain and the rest of the Navy to get even with us, but there was no way around this one. The second station atop hatch four was short arms inspection, followed by a jump to the weather deck, then a trot up a ladder, past the officers' mess to the bridge, down the ladder to the weather deck to hatch three. Here we had to bend over and grasp our ankles while a corpsman looked up our . . . name and address. Then to the bow where we got some shots. The line of Marines, totally naked except for combat boots and iron helmets, extended the entire length of the ship. Oh, the ignominy of it all.

Had a Jap submarine fired a torpedo, it would have missed . . . its crew rendered helpless by fits of giggling would have a hard time explaining it back in Tokyo.

Chapter 6: Don't look conspicuous; it draws fire

When we finally neared the Marianas Islands, we could smell them from far out at sea. We spotted smoke in the mountains of Saipan and heard the dull booming of cannon fire. Our guys had already hit the beach some days before. We were told we would go in as infantry, as most of our battalion tractors had been destroyed. I figured that meant right to the front line. Just for insurance, I walked boldly into the galley, lifted a dozen hard-boiled eggs and concealed them in my gas mask bag.

With rifles and combat packs, we descended loading nets into a bobbing *LCVP*.

Action at last!

The sun was hot, but we didn't care. We stood all hyped up, rifles at the ready, bayonets fixed, eager to charge down the ramp and attack the enemy.

The coxswain steered the boat in a circle, then another and again. What was the matter with him? The damn island was right there! He circled for more than an hour. Finally he got a radio message and headed the stupid boat in the wrong direction, not to Saipan but to Tinian, another island to the south. That, too, was a long trip. I got tired of standing. I looked for something soft to sit on, and I used my gas mask bag. Damn, I'd forgotten about the eggs.

As we approached the reef surrounding Tinian, a couple of artillery shells plopped in the water about fifty yards ahead. This was more like it; we're making a landing. Hot dog!

Admiral Turner, in charge of Fifth Fleet's amphibious operations, wanted to strike on the southwest side of the island at Tinian town. It was fortified and would have been murder. Marine General Holland (Howlin' Mad) Smith, on the other hand, reasoned that, since Saipan lay only three miles across the channel, why not launch the invasion force from there and hit the north end of Tinian? He felt correctly, though the landing areas were small. The Japanese would not expect a blow from the north.[1]

Smith was right, and our men met only light machine gun and rifle fire. By nightfall the entire division was ashore, with only 15 killed and 225 wounded. We lost one man to a mine; well-liked Gibson Oxley. One of our tractors flipped and sank. Everyone except the driver got out. He remained trapped in an air bubble in the dark, inverted cab for almost 45 minutes before slight buoyancy allowed him to crawl from beneath the monster to the surface. He told me he intended to use his .45 rather than suffocate.

Organized resistance on Tinian ceased around August 2. American losses numbered 2000 killed or wounded. The Japanese lost 5000 to 9000. Like Saipan, many of the enemy hid in the jungle, and more than 500 were killed in the next five months at a cost of 38 Marines dead, 125 wounded.

Our coxswain got another radio message. He turned around and headed back toward Saipan. What is going on? This is a combat mission? Action at last ... or last to the action? We were all geared up to do some fighting and then . . . nothing! What a dumb war. Why this strange turn of events? Were we a feint, designed to draw Japs to the wrong side of the island while our guys hit the other side? The feint off Tinian Town was a success but costly. The battleship *Colorado* suffered 22 hits from three 6 inch batteries in 15 minutes. *Colorado* responded and neutralized the batteries but in the meantime she had 43 killed, ten of whom were Marines and 198 wounded which included 32

---

[1] White beach 1 on Tinian was unusually small, about 65 yards wide, making it very difficult for tractors to maneuver. White beach 2 was better, about 120 yards wide. Company E, 2nd Btn., 24th Marines, 4th Div. came in on 1; the 25th landed on 2. Half the troops had to land on a rocky ledge and wade in.

Marines. The destroyer *Norman Scott* lost her skipper along with 18 of her crewmen killed and 47 wounded. Serious enough, but the ruse was considered a complete success.

I guess it worked. Then someone said the Japs had already given up and we weren't needed. Typical erroneous scuttlebutt.

"Yeah, if they gave up, who the hell was shooting at us?" came the retort.

"Well, Japs are just as dumb as Marines . . . there's always some stupid bastard that never gets the word." Possibly the fire never came from Tinian at all but from Aguijan, a smaller island not too far away.

Our arrival at Saipan was hardly noticed. A lot of our wrecked tractors were spread around. The 5th carried in the 10th artillery and the 6th regiment of the 2nd Division, all vets of Tarawa. Again they took a beating and again they dished it out. And again, right from the start, things went wrong.

Naval gunners on the newer ships lacked experience in shore bombardment techniques. Much of their fire was ineffective. Gunners on the veteran ships were far better, but they had only one day to blast their targets, and Saipan was a big island.

Though we landed on a secured beach, fierce fighting was still going on to the north at Marpi Point. Jeeps carrying dead and wounded crawled past us to the nearby field hospital where I would soon be a patient. We straggled past the junk piles of a major portion of 5th and 2nd armored tractors toward a massive, ruined sugar mill. Beyond lay an area where a tank battle had raged. Tanks, both theirs and ours, lay all about.

I heard later that one of the Jap tanks had lain doggo until our first waves passed. It then came to life. It caused a lot of damage until a couple of 5th Amph men stopped it with a bazooka. Unfortunately, I don't know who they were.[2]

---

[2] Later, when I sketched that tank, I pried off the manufacturer's plate. It now hangs on my office wall.

Enemy dead were all around

Eagan[3] and I bivouacked in a muddy area on the side of a small hill. There were enemy dead all around. We cleared an area and shared our shelter halves to make a small tent. It rained all night. The mosquitoes ate us alive while the tent sagged into the mud. We draped the soggy shelter halves around our shoulders, squatted in the mud and let the mosquitoes chew away. In the morning, we moved away from the rest of the group and set up in a shell-battered building with one wall left standing. We draped a canvas from the wall, put our blankets underneath, set up rocks for a cooking area and started housekeeping. We lived here for about two weeks. We didn't erect netting against mosquitoes and soon built up immunity to their bite.

Headquarters, plus "A" and "B" companies, had made the invasion, and the men were only too happy to rest up. They told us that on D-day, after leaving the *LSTs*, they had to bob around for hours; the troops got very sick. Eventually they moved to the line of departure and the signal was given to start the 4000-yard run to the island. But before the beach was gained, the tractors had to cross a dangerously exposed barrier reef 700 yards offshore.

When our naval gunfire ceased, *SBD-3* bombers and Wildcat fighters roared in and peppered the defenses with bombs and .50-caliber and 20mm fire. Seven hundred and nineteen tractors, about half of which were Army units, eventually carried eight battalions of Marines ashore. *LVT-A-4s* of our 2nd Amph Armored unit led the way. Their tractors were the old *LVT-2s* outfitted with a turret and armed with a 75mm pack howitzer. They were called armored, but only the turret deserved that title. Expended casings from our attacking planes

---

[3] B. K. Eagan, a farm boy from Neskoro, Wisconsin, readily admitted to being only a simple country boy. I knew when anyone said that, put both hands on your wallet and run like hell. There was no doubt we would get along. We became close friends.

plummeted down on the advancing waves . . . the heavy brass clanging off helmets and armor caused considerable confusion.

The night before the invasion Japanese gunners placed ranging markers where they felt the tractors would cross. They had done their work well. They were very accurate. However, dense smoke from their own shells soon covered the field of fire, and many of our men were spared.

Earliest estimates of Japanese strength set the figure at 9 to 10,000 troops. This figure was revised upward in early June to between 15 to 18,000. Actually, General Yoshitsuga Saito had 25,469 Imperial Army men and 6,150 Navy personnel.

In addition to the western shore batteries facing our men, General Saito accurately positioned his eastern Magicienne Bay batteries to fire over the island onto our invasion force.

Japanese artillery on Tinian, only three miles away, added considerably to the carnage.

An "A" company tractor carrying Lt. Col. Bill Jones made a clanging approach to Red Beach 2. An enemy tank zeroed in. Lt. Harry Elliott, our liaison officer to the 6th and veteran of the 1st Amphibs of Guadalcanal, was killed instantly, as was his crew. Covered with their blood, Jones made it ashore unscathed.

A gap of over 200 yards caused by Navy guide boats drifting too far to the north developed between the 2nd and 4th Divisions. It took some time to close this dangerous situation. Burning tractors, some loaded with exploding 75mm ammo, added considerably to the confusion, but by 0900 some 8,000 marines were ashore and thousands more were on the way.

Each new load of men and material meant that one of our tractors must again run the gauntlet of fierce cannon and mortar fire. One of our crew chiefs, half exposed above the tractor cab while giving the driver directions, received painful blisters when a hot 47mm shell passed under his armpit between his rib cage and bicep. It blistered the hell out of him. As always, close calls in combat are joked about later. This was about as close as one can get, and it was no joke.

Capt. Bill Stoll, accompanied by Lt. Col. George Shell of the 2nd Btn, came in with the 10th Artillery to join the 75mm pack howitzers just below Charan Kanoa airstrip. Heavy fire rained down immediately, but the 75s already in place blasted back effectively.

The next day was different. A Jap spotter in the heights, possibly in the smokestack of the sugar mill, called very accurate coordinates, and three of the twelve 75s were knocked out. Col. Shell ordered Stoll back to the ship for additional supplies. Stoll barely crawled away before more fire severely wounded the colonel.

D-Day plus 4

About D+4, a Zero screaming over with guns blazing sent our men scrambling. Everyone with a weapon took shots. Gus Paris opened up with a .50 caliber. He missed, he said, by several miles. Angry with himself and unhappy with the catcalls from his comrades, he determined to do better.

He waited for another run. Estimating the direction of approach, he fired a steady stream of lead into the sky, anticipating the plane to fly directly into it. That didn't work either. Machine guns are not built to fire long bursts, but Gus didn't know this, nor did he know why Gunny Sgt. Sam Small rolled on the ground laughing his butt off while the .50 got so hot the barrel burned up. Presumably the Zero pilot returned home safely. Obviously the 5th Amphs weren't taught aerial gunnery.

Nuts like myself and Eagan, I always called him Ege or Eeg, listened to these stories and felt grossly cheated for being left out of the invasion. And now, the battle for Saipan was winding down. Organized resistance soon ceased, but there were hundreds of Japanese still holed up in the jungle and in caves, ready and able to initiate guerrilla raids.

The vets of our battalion had a simple solution: If you want 'em, go get 'em. I was determined to perfect my hard-earned jungle fighting abilities. Well, now, I had the chance, Ege and I stuck close together. When not on regular patrols, we used our free times to make forays into the hills.

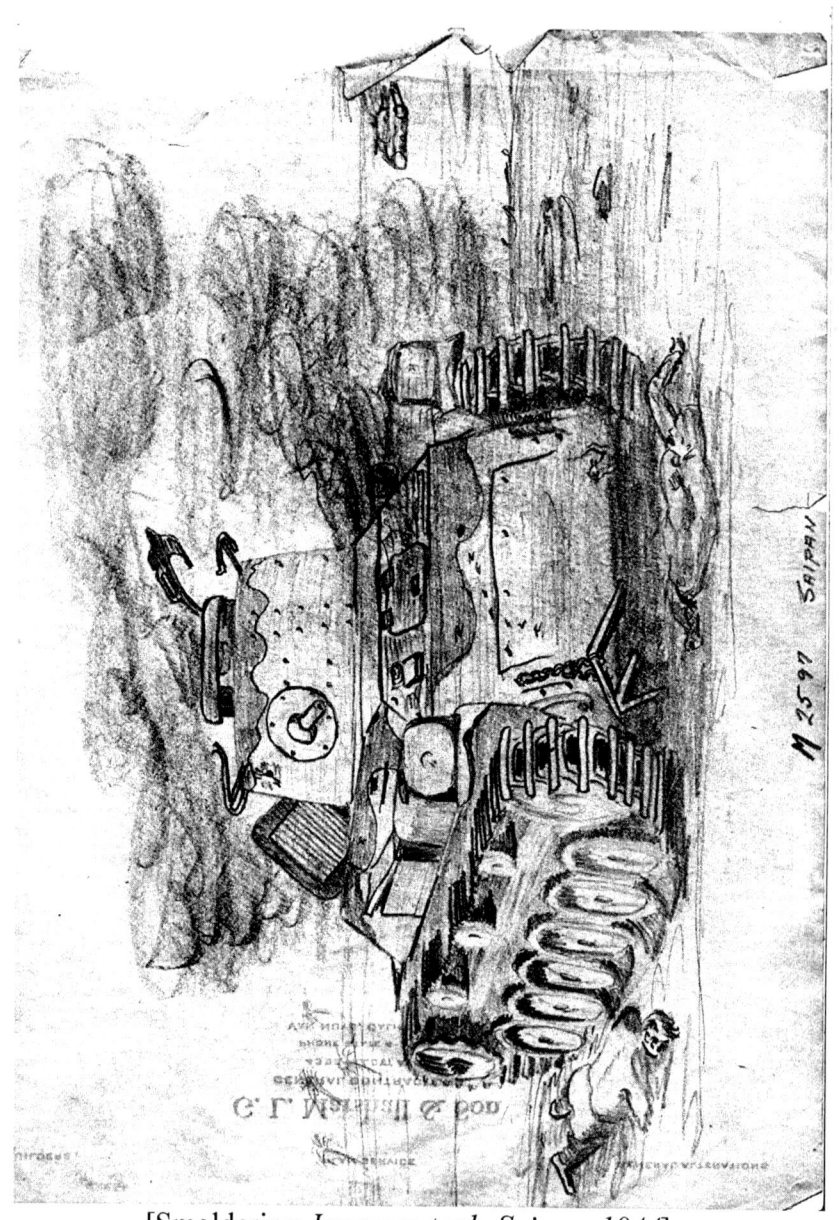

[Smoldering *Japanese tank, Saipan, 1944*]

Chapter 7: How the 5th saved the life of General McArthur and helped sink a Japanese aircraft carrier

The tropical clime of the beautiful Marianas was clean, sweet and warm with plenty of palms, clean water and an abundance of gentle breezes. But before we could enjoy ourselves, broken war equipment had to be cleared away and bodies buried. I could only imagine the chaos as I examined these wrecked tractors with my dead buddies slumped over the controls . . . engines roaring, tractors veering off at crazy angles, tracked grousers clawing into coral or sand, the water stained with blood, oil, and human debris. Equipment discarded by men swimming for their lives littered the lagoon bottom.

Sam Nuzzo's tractor was one of the unfortunates. His crew and passengers were killed or wounded by mortar fire. Sam swam to a wounded, sinking Marine and buoyed him with life preservers. Though suffering from severe gasoline burns, Sam held the man above water for three hours while dodging bullets and incoming assault waves before rescue. Sam was awarded the Navy/Marine Corps medal. I felt guilty enjoying the fruits of their labor by my late arrival on the island.

Sam is a quiet, likable sort of guy, and, like many combat veterans, there are some experiences he would rather not talk about. For example, the time he *killed* his very first Jap.

It seems that he, Bill "the Hooker" Hook, and "Crazy Mex" Demerio Jaure, of B company were scouting the town of Charon Kanoa. No reason, Sam explained, just horsing around, when they came upon an enemy soldier hiding in the weeds. Sam led the trio. With great care he removed his entrenching tool and quick as a flash brought it down on the mid-section of the unsuspecting Japanese. There was a loud "pop," a sudden overwhelming stench, followed by a rain of rotten viscera and numerous ripe body parts.

Was the Jap booby-trapped? Not really, but in a manner of speaking he was. He had been dead for about a week and was grossly bloated, something that Sam, in his zeal to make his very first kill, had overlooked. The sharp entrenching tool effectively released the gas pressure. Crazy Mex received the largest portion of the gooey blast, but the Hooker got some, too. Both immediately swore they were going to make their very first kill too, and it sure as Hell wasn't going to be no dead Jap!

Salvaging *LVTs*

Lt. Early Anderson and his crew did much of the heavy clean-up work. They slaved for several weeks salvaging *LVTs*. Only minimal repairs were made before shipping them back to Hawaii or the States for reconditioning or salvage. Holes were plugged, tracks connected and armor straightened just enough to make them able to float. The tractors were then cabled in line, bow to stern, and towed to waiting cargo ships.

On one occasion four tractors were tethered and towed by two *LVTs* to an AKA cargo ship waiting to boom them aboard. A work party of sailors from the ship stood by to assist. Anderson climbed aboard and ordered the men to sit and not move until he came back. The lieutenant was gone for quite a while. The leaky tractors began taking on water. The work crew noticed what was happening, but they had been ordered to sit, and sit they did.

An urgent call on the ship's loudspeaker woke Anderson in the wardroom. The red-faced officer arrived at the ship's rail just in time to watch the little flotilla of gurgling Alligators slip one after the other into the placid waters.

Stories of the Saipan suicides and murders were spread far and wide

Securing the island of Saipan was a necessary step toward the eventual assault against the Japanese mainland. U.S. bombardments and air strikes began June 11, 1944. The shoreline from Mutcho Point to Agingan Point, six miles south, was severely pounded. Unfortunately, the area included two pretty little towns, Garapan and Charan Kanoa. The brass wanted to preserve Garapan, but the Japanese would have none of that. No doubt, a number of civilians were killed or wounded in these bombardments. In addition to the Japanese military and civilians, there were Chamoro natives, Formosa and Korean workers, Kanakas and even one or two Spaniards. In all, they numbered above 20,000. Most of these innocents had been taught since birth to hate and fear the cannibalistic Marines, who, they were told, had to prove they had murdered their mother and father in order to become Marines.

In anticipation of the attack, Saipan authorities assembled some 1,700 members of Japanese families for evacuation back to Japan aboard the transport ship *America Maru*. Just north of Saipan, the American submarine *Nautilus* torpedoed and sank two vessels of the three-ship convoy. Unfortunately, the *America Maru* was one of them. Many of the elderly, plus women and children, drowned. The sad event added much fuel to the anti-American sentiments of those who remained on the island.

As the Marines advanced, an increasing number of civilians chose suicide over capture. Entire families hurled themselves from the cliffs at Marpi Point. Some frantic parents, misguided by horror stories, beheaded their children before clutching grenades to their chests. Thousands of these poor souls died needlessly.

By July 9, the battle for Saipan ended, for all intents and purposes. About 15,000 civilians listened to the pleading of Japanese-speaking Marines, gave themselves up and were safely interned. Some say at least the same amount perished. Seventeen hundred military prisoners were taken; about 28,000 fighting men died. Marines suffered 16,525 killed or wounded. The U.S. Army reported 3,591 KIA or wounded. In spite of the fierceness of the fighting, and given that the Marines were just as determined as the Japanese, I know of no abuse against non-combatants by Americans. Marines, in particular, went out of their way to care for civilians, especially the little kids.

Stories of the Saipan suicides and murders were spread far and wide by the media in the States. Photos and movies graphically depicted these atrocities. Concerned parents immediately wondered ... if the Japanese committed horrible acts upon their own people, what were they doing to our boys?

The only time Baldy was beat.

Our exec, Capt. Stoll, had the depressing task of writing to the next of kin of those who had fallen. One day, while seated in headquarters tent, taking care of correspondence, a letter of concern arrived from a frantic mother and her daughter.

"My son," the mother wrote, "a private in your organization, has not been heard from since the 5th left for overseas. Is he dead, injured, or, worse yet, captured?"

Bill (Baldy) Stoll was the best problem solver in 5th Amphs and probably the best in the Corps, and he never got beat.

A case in point . . .

The day before the Saipan landing, Baldy, as senior officer aboard one of the *LSTs*, was summoned to sick bay. The doctor informed him of a problem with one of the Alligator drivers.

"He might," said the doc, "be suffering from acute appendicitis. He moans when I touch him but moans in all the wrong places."

"He's a good man," Baldy said. "He just needs a bit of help. Prep him as usual, but don't let on what I want you to do . . . ."

The gurney was wheeled under the bright lights, the groaning patient prepped. A grim-faced, gown-clad corpsman entered the O.K., carrying a tray of instruments. He tripped. Scalpels, forceps and sponges fell to the deck. The corpsman retrieved the items, carefully wiped each piece on his sleeve and replaced it on the tray. Then he sneezed,

That was the signal for the captain and the sober-faced doctor to enter. Ignoring his sniffling assistant, the medic informed Stoll they were short of anesthetic. Could more be found? He would hate to perform surgery without anesthetic. Stoll said he would try, and left. While lighting a cigar, the doctor assured the ill Marine that everything would be all right.

The doc was brushing ashes from his gown when Stoll returned with the news that there was no problem. The chief engineer was rigging a hose to pipe up some carbon monoxide. It would do in a pinch. However, the gas must be carefully monitored lest some serious consequences result.

The Alligator man recovered immediately and carried out his duties the following day. The incident was never again mentioned. Now, Captain Stoll had a worried mother to console. Easy enough, thought Stoll. Simply remind the boy to write home more often.

The captain summoned the private and was surprised to learn the lad had no wish to communicate with his family. Somewhat chagrined, the captain wrote and informed the mother and sister of the situation. They, however, were not to be put off so easily.

They wrote back, "... something terrible has happened to our loved one and you are purposely keeping the horrible news from us."

Stoll again summoned the man to his tent and was again informed that there was no wish to communicate, the private adding that he did not like to write.

The following month another frantic and even more accusatory letter arrived. Exasperated, Stoll put out the word for the man to report to him immediately! On the double! Now!

"By God," Stoll rumbled, "you write to your mother or face disciplinary action!"

A few days later the captain short-stopped the outgoing mail for compliance and censorship. He found the following: "The captain told me I had to write so I am. Now mind your own damn business!"

This was the only time Baldy was beat.

Easing the tension

Capt. Bill Clark remembered D-day, Saipan, very well. Our tractors had 10th Artillerymen and equipment aboard. Everyone was waiting for the signal to debark.

"Tension was so thick," Clark wrote, "you could cut it with a knife. Suddenly a 10th master sergeant jumped and started playing a Ping-Pong game with himself, all the while making humorous comments regarding good or bad imaginary shots. Soon he had everyone laughing. Even me.

Stoll and Clark later complimented the sergeant for defusing the situation.

"What the Hell," commented the man, "I went through this once before on Tarawa and thought maybe I could help the situation a bit."

Eagan and I gladly helped with the clean up. We picked up a lot of usable and salable items from the bottom inside the reef. About a hundred yards from the beach, just beyond a drowned Sherman tank, we discovered an *SBD* bomber in fairly good condition. Already, it offered a home to a multitude of colorful fish. We rigged a diving apparatus from a gas mask, a garden hose and a bicycle pump and appropriated an out-rigger canoe. One of us stayed aboard and pumped while the other struggled beneath the surface to remove the propeller. We planned on selling it to one of the Army or Navy units setting up camp on the island. A prop like that would make a good entry display. We failed, but we managed to bring up a parachute.

We decided to sell genuine Japanese flags to the newcomers. We cut the silk into three-foot squares on which we painted red rising suns. The results were so awful even the Navy wouldn't buy them, and they usually bought anything. Another moneymaking scheme was foiled, but the swimming was great and only occasionally was it interrupted by a bloated body drifting in.

Many of our companions were avid fishermen. In the absence of fly rods, grenades served just as well. Of course, there were some that didn't think it sporting, but lots of fish were consumed, and apparently none was of the poisonous fugu or puffer fish variety, since nobody complained of a belly ache or keeled over dead.

There were other methods of obtaining seafood, unorthodox perhaps, but not unwelcome.

Marvin Mann, of B Company, had a tractor with chronic severe engine trouble. No amount of service or reconditioning by our able mechanics effected a cure. After numerous requests, a new engine finally arrived from Hawaii aboard a ship docked at Tanapag. Mann and his crew raced to the waterfront. While the crane operator's attention was focused on retrieving the engine from the ship's hold, one of the tractor men discovered an interesting crate seeping hazy wisps from dry ice just out of everyone else's line of vision. Fearing it a devilish incendiary device secreted by Japanese infiltrators, our Alligator men heroically risked their lives to load the crate aboard their truck. Concealing it under a tarp, their prize was brought back to camp and opened. It contained pounds and pounds of frozen lobster, oysters and salmon. Someone opined that it must have been en route to General Douglas MacArthur. No doubt, the enemy plotted to poison him.

We ate it all, just in case it might have been contaminated or something.

No, they didn't forget the engine.

The 5th and their habit of borrowing

It is hard to say exactly when the 5th got into the habit of borrowing materials from other organizations. All borrowed items were honestly intended to be paid back just as soon as the war ended or thereabouts. The first incident of which I am aware occurred when our unit was forming at the boat basin. If one of the few tractors assigned us broke down, we were helpless. We had neither tools nor spare parts. Everything was being shipped to active units overseas. High on our priority list was a portable machine shop. Sharp-eyed Gunny Pierce located one at Pendleton and immediately assembled a work party. He invited battalion maintenance officer Capt. Bill Clark along. Clark figured they needed him to lend a semblance of legality. The Alligator men crossed the highway, The M.P.s at the Pendleton gate dutifully saluted Lt. Clark and our conspirators were in.

Within an hour of the successful raid, Capt. Stoll received a phone call from a very angry maintenance officer promising dire punishment to the offenders. Stoll calmly explained the gunny had merely read the wrong acquisition papers, pulled into the wrong storage area and hooked up to the wrong portable machine shop, innocently assuming it was the one promised us; if there was any problem the item would be returned.

I don't know what part of the country that officer came from, but he believed every word!

It was a dry run but good practice for the future.

Ingenuity of the 5th really came to the front on Saipan, when we acquisitioned truck loads of lumber to build wooden decks for our tents. Not even divisional headquarters was so blessed. Intercoms, too, appeared magically and were installed in each tent . . . donated by the Santa Claus Division, in case anyone asked. With this luxury, we now listened to Rose broadcasting from Tokyo. Rose knew us better than we thought.

How the 5th saved General McArthur

She always called us boneheads. Later on, we had our own radio station on Saipan, but hers was better.

The 5th always ate well. Unlike many units, our cooks, to their undying credit, knew what they were doing.

One night on requisition detail at a newly formed but poorly guarded food dump, we were busy heisting cases of turkey, beef and fruit cocktail when we met a few Japanese stragglers performing the same task. They remained at the far end of the row. They quietly picked up what they could and left. We did the same ... no sense in starting a fuss since none of us was authorized to be there ... it was an Army food dump!

It wasn't long before every service on the island complained of missing refrigerators, missing plumbing, missing everything. We couldn't understand why. We had a surplus of all of these items.

It was rumored that Lt. Walt Sonnenberg was a water dowser. I didn't know about that, but our tree-dangling Lister bags were soon replaced by newly painted 300-gallon water trailers. He must have been a good plumbing dowser, too, because he dowsed pipe, faucets and shower heads. We were soon luxuriating with soap and fresh water. No doubt some bewildered supply officer on the other side of the island could only blame his losses on those thieving Japanese infiltrators.

One sunny day Emory Prine of Yreka, California, and some others left on foot toward Charon Kanoa. Before long, they returned with a canopied truck . . . Army issue, probably. The numbers were quickly painted over. They asked me to come along on a special detail. I was slated for guard duty and declined. Later that afternoon the truck returned in a cloud of dust, skidded around the corner and sped to the rear of the compound. Curious as to what they had acquired, I sidled over. It was, of all things, a piano! Where it came from or how they got it, who knew? I doubt that any of our men knew how to play, but nevertheless the 5th had a real piano.

When notified that nearby Army and Navy units added a minimum of 20 percent to all their requisitions just to cover losses, Major Shead took the implied charges of thievery very seriously.

"I will conduct," he announced, "a full investigation of the matter . . . soon."

Word of my bare feet got back to the States

However resourceful our Marines were, they were at a loss to replace my worn-out size 15 combat boots. Had the Army or Navy stocked boots or shoes that size, I'm certain Capt. Wilgus or Quartermaster Sgts. Crummitt and Crase or Helgeson, Ed Barnes or any of my buddies would had picked them up. To them, it became a challenge. The problem really didn't bother me. Going barefoot developed calluses tough enough to strike kitchen matches on.

Somehow, word of my bare feet got back to the States. A women's group and a bunch of preachers started a campaign, "Bring that poor boy home!" they crowed. Going home was not an option for me. The pressure kept up. Finally, Lt. Joe Reece came into the tent one night and offered me a trip stateside, or at least to Hawaii, for the remainder of the war.

"No," I refused. Others in the tent looked on with astonishment and envy. Reece was dumbfounded.

A few days later I stumbled across a dozen or so Jap combat boots. Too small for me, of course, but I managed to obtain enough leather and laces to sew and tie something together that vaguely resembled shoes. I carefully screwed hobnails into the soles and built up the heels. The stupid things did nothing but raise blisters on top of blisters. I threw them away and went back to my barefoot status and prayed those dopey women in the States would shut up. Then one blessed day in early February, a B-29 arrived from Hawaii with my size 15 boots. How our supply people did it, was beyond me.

"every God damn spare part on the God damn island"

It is safe to say there were more fictitious requisition papers, orders and ranks floating about Saipan, courtesy of 5th Amphs, than of any other unit on the American side. Not even the Japanese could match us in the art of deception. In addition to normal supplies, our armory and even our motor pool increased by leaps and bounds.

A company jeep almost got me into trouble. The jeep, formerly owned by the U.S. Navy, was painted with the standard navy gray or light blue. Somehow it strayed into our area and received a coat of Marine green. For months it served us well. Then, one day it broke down on the road between Garapan and Charon Kanoa. A mechanic was summoned. Unfortunately he was not of our unit. He noted the underside of the hood clearly bore the original color. The MPs questioned the driver and occupants. One of them in a mischievous mood told them to ask Marshall.

The MPs arrived at my tent. I, of course, being completely innocent, told them that on the day the vehicle was supposedly stolen some months before, I was Jap hunting in the hills. To prove it, I produced one or two rifles, miscellaneous Jap paraphernalia, several skulls, and some gold teeth. For whatever reason, they dropped the matter. Whoever fingered me remained a mystery.

Someone returned to camp with a lot of packaged radio parts that had been left lying around. By coincidence, on Nov. 9, 1944, the submarine *ArcherFish SS 311* arrived at Maniagassa Island at Tanapag harbor with radio problems. Sub Commander Joe Enright requested the location of the needed parts. He was informed he should contact the 5th Amphibs. "They can fix anything because they have every God damn spare part on the God damn island."

Lt. Ernie Chase heard of the submariner's need and volunteered Paris, Prorak and Polack to solve the problem. The three experts found the vessel's transmitter needed relays of the same type they just happened to have. The trio not only repaired the equipment but offered several spare relays, just in case. They were angling for a ride in the sub, but, due to patrol commitments, their request was turned down. However, the grateful commander offered ten gallons of ice cream to soothe the disappointed jarheads.

ArcherFish left on her patrol. A week or so later, she scored a major victory, the only sinking of her career. It was Japan's secret supership, the *Shinano, a* 59,000-ton aircraft carrier, its hull based on the blueprints of the battleship *Yamato.* The *Shinano* was the largest warship sunk by submarine during WWII.[1]

Once again the Alligator men of the 5th Amphtracs saved the day!

---

[1] Report of U.S. Technical Mission to Japan, 1946: "Of all naval catastrophes, from the Japanese point of view, the loss of the Shinano was the most depressing. The third and last of the super warships, she was sunk on the second day of her maiden cruise, by only four submarine torpedoes. The shock which went through the Japanese Naval Ministry is better imagined than described."

Chapter 8: When you have secured an area, don't forget to tell the enemy

Saipan had fallen, yet hundreds of Japanese soldiers, sailors and civilians refused to surrender. Living in small enclaves concealed by heavy foliage in the canyons and hills, the intransigents eked out a marginal existence. Capt. Sakae Oba, Imperial Japanese Army, eventually organized men and women into a quasi-military force, which kept up harassment raids on the Americans for more than a year after the fall of the island and for some months after the defeat of Japan.

Operationally they posed no threat to us, but individually they proved quite deadly. A wire stretched across a road was a favorite way to decapitate jeep drivers; mines planted in roads and paths created severe hazards. Infiltrators tossing grenades into airplane cockpits at Isley field and into ammo dumps around the island always kept guards on their toes.

One of our "A" company *LVTs* came clanking into the tractor park sporting a newly attached Japanese magnetic anti-tank mine just above the second and third bogie wheels. The mine, a hand-thrown device with a ten-second fuse, fortunately, failed to work. The crew had no idea where they picked it up or how long they had been banging around with it.

Snipers were always a problem and could strike at any time. One innovative Japanese carried a Wakizashi short sword and developed a nasty habit of concealing himself alongside a path to ambush a lone American. At the proper moment, he leaped up and, in a quick twisting motion, disemboweled his victim, and then disappeared into the foliage.

This guy became my personal mission and the goal of many of my jungle raids. I *wanted* that Wakizashi. I *wanted* the Jap. I got neither.

We heard of three Navy ensigns and three nurses who jeeped too far into the hills on a sightseeing tour. They were ambushed. The ensigns' heads were stuck on poles alongside the road. The nurses, staked out and raped, died, too.

We went searching for those Japs. We planned on moving fast, so carried only carbines and grenades. Some fellows from 2nd Armored came up with an *LVT-A-4* tank. They circled and found some supply caves. They blasted them shut with their 75 mm. It was unclear if any of the enemy were immediately killed, but we managed to flush a few.

[We heard about a jeep that was ambushed with the nurses staked out and raped. We went after them]

Eagan let out a yelp. Five or six Japs rushed from the jungle toward us; Eagan picked off one. Then the damned clip dropped from his carbine before he could fire again. I sighted in on the next charging man. He suddenly changed direction and headed for deep jungle. My round brought him down, but the expended brass jammed in the bolt. As I hammered frantically on the action lever, Aaron Riddle hurled a grenade. The grenade hit a low branch, bouncing back. We scrambled in one direction; the enemy in the other while the grenade exploded harmlessly.

When you have secured an area, don't forget to tell the enemy

Whether or not they were the ones who killed those Navy people, we felt better, even if we shot only two.

Oba's people eventually surrendered after the war and then only with reluctance. The captain stated that one of his men, Pvt. Horiuchi, scored more than forty-five American kills between the fall of Saipan from July of '44 to July of '45, when he, Horiuchi, was trapped and killed by Marines.

Had a man named Horiuchi been one of the ones we got? None of 'them' had names for us, just Jap faces. We seldom saw the reality of the enemy as people with families and everyday lives like us. There were exceptions, of course, like when I stumbled across a finely Grafted suit of medieval Japanese armor, complete with winged helmet. A bit off the trail, it lay propped against a tree, left there, no doubt, by some family who had cherished it for generations and later hoped to retrieve it. The armor shone beautifully. If only I could have rescued it from the elements. Barring that, one could only hope that somehow it returned in good condition to its original owner.

The Easter Egg Kid and other lucky breaks

Not all my forays into the hills were successful in terms of killing the enemy. Some of my adventures were funny, others downright scary. In retrospect, I suppose all were rather stupid.

I recall one lucky break when a grenade landed at my feet, hurled from some place in the jungle. I did not hear the telltale "pop" we learned about in Raider school, but I did hear the fizz of the fuse, followed by a weak-sounding "woof." Japanese grenades were quite deadly, but, occasionally, a defective one burst into hundreds of tiny fragments the size of sand grains, while another blew out one end and left the grenade looking like an open tin can. The missile that landed at my feet split in half like a cantaloupe. The unexploded picric acid charge covered me in a bright yellow cloud. My dungarees, plus my exposed face and hands, turned a brilliant yellow. For weeks they dubbed me "the Easter Egg Kid." This kind of dumb luck is what gets a Marine in trouble . . . he begins to think he is grenade and bulletproof. The easter egg lesson was lost on me as well as Eagan.

Marpi Point had been taken but not occupied. Nobody wanted it until much later in the year. Eagan and I were up there fooling around one bright day, watching an armed patrol winding along a trail some distance from us. Thinking they were our people, we waved. Obviously they had the same thoughts as they waved back. It was only then we noticed the peculiar shape of their pith helmets. They were Japanese!

We ducked into the brush and found a track similar to a rabbit run. We crawled a hundred feet or so through the thick banyan roots and kunai grass. Sunlight shown through the greenery as I lead our way. Shushing Eagan, I inched forward toward a small clearing about ten feet in diameter. My head poked through the leaves and there, perched on a boulder, its eyes looking directly into mine, sat a huge lizard. It was an iguana or a monitor . . . or a Komodo dragon, for all I knew. Its claws were as big as small bananas and its tongue flicked out about a foot, it looked to me that its fangs were dripping yellow poison. Not only that it had mean eyes filled with hate and it intended rip me into little bitty pieces and eat me.

Frozen on the trail, Ege rammed his helmeted head into my rear, urging me on. No way! Directly behind the rock and lizard stood a Japanese soldier! The startled Jap looked down at me. I, equally startled, looked up at him. Eagan cursed and pushed again. I couldn't back up. Quite honestly, the Jap displayed more presence of mind than I. He coolly raised a finger to his lips and motioned silence. Dumb me, I obeyed! Then, without a word or hostile move, the soldier turned and disappeared into the jungle. The lizard did the same. The impatient Eagan butted me hard, and I sprawled into the clearing.

It was difficult to figure out exactly what in the hell happened. Eagan alleged I had been *suckered*.

When you have secured an area, don't forget to tell the enemy

[I had become calloused toward death and bones. Our makeshift quarters are to the right.]

Terror is a cold, damp, suffocating blanket

Fright is a relative term. We all experience fright at one time or another and are usually not afraid to admit it. A person can be frightened silly by an encounter with a wild animal, a near miss in traffic or a barrage of artillery and still perform an assigned task. Terror, however, is a completely different matter. Terror cannot be explained. It can only be sensed. It is a sensation that deprives one of all rational thought. Terror envelops the entire being in a cold, damp, suffocating blanket.

This day, I crept through the brush alongside a trail, a slow but safe method when alone in questionable territory. The path inclined slightly, eventually leading to a series of stone steps. The steps ended at a colonnaded edifice supporting a colorful, ornate roof. Capriciously, I happened upon a beautiful little Shinto shrine tucked away in the deep jungle and surrounded by sweet-smelling plumeria, mangrove and liana. Colorful birds danced from branch to branch, their song mingling with the humming of numerous insects. The beauty of the place presented a totally unexpected pastoral scene. Intending to take a swig from my canteen, I stood, then froze mid-way when I spotted the skeleton.

It was human, seated in an attitude of repose a few steps below the shrine. The bones, except for a few scraps of cloth, were picked clean. Skeletons on this island of death were common. I had become calloused toward death and bones. Most of us had--we had to in order to stay sane. We had rings carved from bones and collections of skulls for trading purposes. I even wore a gold tooth necklace--something my Dad would not have approved of. Most of the thousands of Japanese dead had simply been bulldozed into huge ditches.

But this was different, a moment torn from time and space encapsulated in a surrealistic blink between life and death. I pictured this person, mortally wounded, crawling to this place of refuge to die in the comforting embrace of his God. Within a few steps of his goal, he rested, never to move again. One elbow supported the hollow frame in an upright position. The empty eye sockets studied me in a reproachful, yet pitying manner. No longer did the friendly bird song or the happy buzz of insects fill the air. There was no sound at all, not even of gunfire from destroyers banging away at the shoreline cliffs below me.

The day became oppressively still, hot and humid. I shivered; while hair on the nape of my neck prickled. If ever there were, as put by Shakespeare, ". . . warnings and portents of evils imminent," this was it!

Not that this place was evil. Quite the contrary. This was a sacred place. This was an unknown dimension occupied by that holy shrine and its brooding sentry. This place *did not want me there.* Sheer terror enshrouded me; death laughed. I inched back into the undergrowth and fled, never to return.

Chapter 9: Anything you do can get you shot. . . including doing nothing

The warrior's code of Bushido, honorable in Japanese eyes, was confusing to Marines. To us, dying in battle is an acceptable, though not sought after, event. It was quite different with the Japanese, and we Marines never could fathom their line of reasoning.

Maniagassa, a small, fortified island in Tanapag harbor, was thought neutralized by naval shelling, but vessels entering and leaving complained of enemy small arms fire. Tractors were in short supply, and several had to be pulled from Susupe swamp with the aid of a reconditioned Jap tank. George Revoir was nearly killed when a cable snapped and almost took off his head. The weather turned bad, and the men wanted to postpone the operation. They finally borrowed some tractors from "B" Company.

Four 2nd Armored tractors led three waves of our tracs. Japanese fire from the island was ineffectual. Two of the enemy tried to leave in a rowboat; everyone fired; all missed. One Jap escaped up the beach. The other was finally cut in half with a Browning Automatic Rifle (BAR). A small, circling observation plane dropped a note saying a Jap was trying to escape by hiding under a floating orange crate. Before the man could be shot, a 2nd Div. Marine waded out, saying he wanted a prisoner. With knife in hand, the Marine approached the box. The Jap threw the box aside, stared at the Marine, then ducked under the water. The tractor men just a few feet away swear he never resurfaced. Apparently he drowned himself. His body was not found.

John Fox, a buddy from Tennessee, recalled another event: *Second Division requested some tracs to go out in Tanapag harbor to knock out a group firing a machine-gun from a reef* and, at the same time, clean out another bunch of Japanese giving us trouble from some fishing boats.

Lt. P. K. Plakias, volunteers 'A' Company, 3rd platoon, to do the job. Three tracs went out, eight men to a tractor plus driver and CP (radio). We were lead tractor. Just as we approached, a Jap wades out from between two high chunks of coral. Our interpreter talks to him, but we can't understand. Just in case, Andy Kovach is fingering a .50 caliber.

We, with our M-1s, are leaning over the sides of the cargo area, which is hard to do unless you are six foot six or something. All of a sudden this nice little Japanese man grabs two hidden grenades and slams them together. He raises back to throw, just like in a ball game. We all duck while Andy saws him in half with the .50.

After this some Japs are seen walking away from us on the other side. The interpreter asks them to surrender. One turns and begins coming back. There were eight; one of these, an officer, comes after the deserter, shouting. The man ignores him and keeps coming our way. Suddenly the officer pulls a sword from behind his back and takes a mighty swing. The man's head drops into the surf. It happened so fast we did not have time to do much about it. The officer than raises the sword in a show of defiance and shook it at us. We gave him a 21-gun salute. The rest of the Japs got the same thing.

We turned around to the boats in the harbor. We found many soldiers who gave their lives for the emperor by putting rifle barrels in their mouths and pulling the trigger with their big toe. Andy was the big hero for the day. Much later he got a field commission and eventually retired from the Corps as a major.

Some 30 prisoners were eventually taken and, in spite of the bombardment and horrid living conditions, all were dressed in clean, white clothes. One older gentleman quipped, "Ten minutes ago me Jap, now me American."

Thus, tiny Maniagassa was cleaned up and used for a submarine base.

An infiltrator spotted

Sgt. Jack Polack tells another story about a Bushido warrior and the damage he caused. Jack says he was tired after hours on the radio, dispatching tractors from ship to shore, each bringing in much-needed food ammo and medical supplies. The Alligator men had been on the move constantly since the initial landing six days before. Tractors moved day and night form ship to shore. 2nd Armored reported their sentries had spotted an infiltrator in the area. Everyone was too busy to worry about a single infiltrator. It was the 21st of June.

Baldy Stoll and several other officers were offshore, handling the unloading of ship after ship. One ship was just about emptied when its confused captain approached and asked Baldy what he should do with the two hundred sleeping cots stored in the aft hold. There seemed to be no paper work, he complained and they had to go to somebody. Stoll, as usual, had the answer.

Within two hours, the cots were ashore, and the tired men of the 5th were bedding down. They couldn't get over it. Real cots, what luxury!

Larry Purcell was so tickled that he removed his boots before turning in, a real no-no in combat. Unfortunately, none of the men paid heed that they were bedding down next to an ammo dump full of 105mm artillery shells.

The first explosion hurled Sgt. Polack through the windshield of the communication jeep. Gus Paris, Ed Stalling and Walk Prorack found themselves and their cots almost 15 yards away, entangled atop a dozen other men of the 5th. Blast after blast hurled live 105mm shells through the night. They, in turn, exploded on impact. Raging flames lit half the island and the many ships in the harbor. There was no way to fight the fire. It had to burn itself out.

A burned and bleeding Marine staggered from the inferno, while a horrified Capt. Nielsen, 10th Artillery, 2nd Div., raced up, begging help for the work party he had just ordered in there. The officer tried to enter but was held back by Gus and Ed. Many men outside were wounded, but all inside, with the exception of the one, were killed. Anyone still able to drive an Alligator ferried the wounded to the hospital ships outside the reef. Most all our guys returned after treatment. As usual, if wounds were not serious enough for a man to be pulled from the line and hospitalized, no Purple Hearts were recommended.

Our men did manage to load themselves down with fresh fruit and, when ashore, gladly shared with others. There was considerable lamenting over the damaged cots though. In the mean time, it took Larry Purcell more than two hours to find his boondockers.

Official records state that a careless Marine caused the explosion, but there was an infiltrator near the dump earlier that evening, as reported by 2nd Armored. They couldn't get a clear shot and lost him. There was no doubt it was he who gave his life for the emperor.

Those American Devils

0800 July 6 1944 Lt. General Saito's last message.

Japanese Officers and men defending Saipan. I am addressing the officers and men of the Imperial Army on Saipan. For more than twenty days since the American Devils attacked, the officers, men and civilian employees of the Imperial Army and Navy on this island have fought well and bravely. Everywhere they have demonstrated the honor and glory of the Imperial Forces. I expected every man would do his duty.

Heaven has not given us an opportunity. We have not been able to utilize fully the terrain. We have fought in unison up to the present time, but now we have no materials with which to fight and our artillery for attack has been completely destroyed. Our comrades have fallen one after another. Despite the bitterness of defeat we pledge, "Seven lives to repay our country."

The barbarous attack of the enemy is being continued. Even though the enemy has occupied only a small corner of Saipan we are dying without avail under the violent shelling and bombing. Whether we attack or whether we stay where we are, there is only certain death. However, in death there is life. We must advance with those who remain to deliver still another blow to the American Devils, and leave our bones on Saipan as a bulwark of the Pacific.

As it says in the "Senjinkun" Battle Ethics, "I will never suffer the disgrace of being taken alive," and "I will offer up the courage of my soul and calmly rejoice in living by the eternal principle."

Here I pray with you for eternal life of the Emperor and the welfare of my country and now I advance to seek out the enemy. "Follow Me."

Saito committed suicide two hours later.

Marines have a motto, *Semper Fidelis*, Always Faithful, and are damn proud of it. As opposed to Bushido, our *esprit de corps* encourages a Marine not only to do his duty but also to remain alive.

[*Surrender leaflet dropped by US flyers*]

Chapter 10: Important things are simple; It's the simple things that are hard

Everyone looked forward to "mail call," the high point of the week, even when the mail barge sank just before Christmas. Eventually salvaged, the barge's contents were wet but our spirits were not dampened. Christmas cookies tasted a little salty, but no one cared. Everyone but Ege and I had girlfriends or wives writing to them. Letters from our relatives were of the, "How are you, we are fine," type, nice but hardly earth shaking.

To any Marine in the Pacific

I did correspond with Theresa Marlaire of Bradley, Illinois. She had addressed a letter to "Any Marine in the Pacific." I got it, and she became a pen pal. Her letters were always sweet, and her picture showed her to be very pretty.

One of our more enterprising buddies had a way with words and would pen such drivel as, "I lay here at night, gazing at the silvery rays of the moon kissing the tops of the rippling waves, they seem to be building a path of love that will remain forever cherished in my thoughts ...," or, "... the aroma of this tropical evening blends with the freshness of your soft skin and the flowers you weave in your golden tresses..." Yecch! The less erudite eagerly sought his ghostwriting services and gladly forked over 25 cents a page. He made a fortune, and I am certain many a sweetie back home sincerely believed each and every word.

Then, there were comedians such as Jack Luncsford, who wrote home, "... there I was, laying in a foxhole, I heard a rustling sound . . . they were getting closer, my heart began to pound. I knew this might be the end of me, but I would go down fighting. Determined to use the element of surprise, I jumped out and faced eight of them. I killed two and wounded at least one. I felt no remorse, after all, this was war! Those damned land crabs had better avoid messing with a United States Marine!"

After a cliffhanger buildup like that, I think the reader would want to kill him.

There was no sense writing on both sides of the paper, as letters were censored, not with a black line, but with a razor blade. They were thoroughly shredded by the time they got home.

One Marine wrote: "Sweetheart, Just a line to let you know I am all right." He followed this with a squiggly line clear to the bottom of the page, where he signed, "Love you, Joe." His attitude? Let them cut something out of that!

A favorite trick of some writers, to confuse not only the censor but also the person to whom the letter was addressed, "... don't forget to look under the stamp." Since no stamps were necessary on outgoing mail, the censor and addressee would go crazy trying to find a secret watermark or traces of invisible ink in the glued portions of the envelope.

Lt. Anderson owed his wife a letter but did not feel like writing. He cut the entire center from a page, leaving only a one-inch border on all four sides. At the top he wrote "Dear Anne," and at the bottom he signed, "Love, Andy,"It appeared our censor, Lt. P. K. Plakias, was the villain.

Anne had met Plakias while the outfit was still stateside, and she immediately recognized his initials on the censor stamp. Two weeks later the innocent and confused P. K. received a scorching letter from Anne concerning his abuse of censorship powers, not only to herself, but to her dear, sweet, ever-loving, letter writing husband!

My ever-increasing scouting and infiltrating abilities were actually worth bragging about. On one occasion, I couldn't resist writing home to let them in on my newly honed skills "... and yesterday I killed two more of them damn Japs."

Important things are simple; It's the simple things that are hard

Expecting the monumental, "Jack Armstrong, All American Boy" type praise, I was rudely shaken some weeks later when I received a scathing letter from my father.

"Donald," he wrote, "you have taken the lives of two of the enemy as you are expected to do. You have done so before and will, no doubt, do so again, but . . . under no circumstances will you rob them of their dignity by calling them 'damn Japs.' Their personal honor and their duty to their country are just as precious to them as your honor and your duty are to you. I will not tolerate any more of that kind of language."

Dad always was pretty high-minded.

[Letter home]

Chapter 11: Make it too tough for the enemy to get in, and you can't get out

The United States Marine Corps is extremely cautious about sanitary conditions. Any infractions, especially while in the field, are dealt with harshly. Our doctors and corpsmen were not Marines but Navy personnel. Nevertheless, what they accomplished under fire and other extreme conditions deserves far more credit than I can give them here.

The first facilities to be erected as soon as battlefield conditions permit are the heads (latrines to Army guys). Heads consist of large wooden boxes covered on top but open beneath. The top has six to eight holes with flop lids. Even with no walls, privacy being least important, these were far better than straddle trenches, which, as the name implies, were used in exactly that manner. Every morning a "head detail" moved the boxes aside, tossed some old motor oil mixed with a pint of gasoline into the pit and torched it.

It was smelly but kept the flies down and the rodents hopping. Life was in the raw until the Army and Navy nurses arrived. Then canvas walls were erected around the heads. This step toward modesty caused at least one embarrassing moment.

A banana grove near our camp was visited only occasionally when the fruit was ripe. The grove offered, however, an ideal place of concealment for a Japanese soldier, one of the few who wanted to surrender. Just how he could accomplish this without getting bullet riddled posed a problem. For days he studied the layout. Each morning after roll and sick call papers were completed and filed, the same officer left the headquarters tent with reading material in hand and made his way to the head.

After the Japanese soldier was certain of the established routine, he settled on a risky plan. Allowing four minutes for the officer to be comfortably seated and, presumably, absorbed in his reading material, the Jap made certain the coast was clear, then dashed across the cleared area, burst through the door, threw up his hands and shouted, "I sullenda! I sullenda!"

The plan was a complete success. Needless to say, the surprised officer, who shall remain nameless, had additional paper work to take care of.

[This picture was routine until we invented the Saipan Maytag!]

The Saipan Maytags

Until the arrival of an Army laundry unit, our dungarees, skivvies and socks were washed by hand until someone devised what we called a Saipan Maytag. It consisted of half a fifty-gallon gasoline drum mounted with a homemade crankshaft and a wooden propeller. The afternoon wind actuated the propeller, which drove coconut shell pistons up and down in the soapy water. Soon, everyone was building a wash machine. We always had clean clothes, but the windmills made camp look like a miniature Dutch landscape.

Tents appeared out of nowhere due to the ingenuity of our procurement people such as Pete Wilgus, Al Snyder and others. Company streets were laid out and lined with whitewashed rocks. There was a beer garden for us and an officers club for the brass. Major Shead had a regular tropical hut built, lined with sandbags.

The local tooth fairy

Dr. Donald Hawkins and our dentist, Dr. Stanaback, along with a crew of first-rate corpsmen, conducted daily inspections and were very conscientious about looking after the welfare of the men. Stanaback had a great reputation as a tooth fairy, and I had a fang that was acting up. I walked into the tent, but when I saw the Rube Goldberg dentist's drill, a bicycle wheel contraption with an arm and a bunch of small pulleys and elbows powered by a bored-looking corpsman pumping the pedals, I decided my tooth didn't hurt at all.

"Nonsense," said Stanaback.

Before I knew it, I was collared and pushed down on a box that substituted for a dental chair. The jammed fingers in my mouth were not my own.

"Aha,! He chortled, "I'll just push this black one out of the way . . . ."

"Unggh, unggh."

"Not to worry. Yes, indeedy, there that little bugger is, right behind all that green stuff. Wow, look at the size of that hole! Come here, Hicks, take a look."

Another finger went in, "See? Right next to the tooth that is fizzing."

Hicks grimaced. Stanaback picked up the brace and bit.

"Nunnggh!"

Hicks returned to the bicycle seat.

"You may start pedaling, Hicks."

The whine of the drill grew closer and louder.

"Gaaack!"

It was no use; my pleas were in vain.

"Now, corporal," his voice was less than soothing, "this might smoke a bit, but don't you pay any attention. I can always throw cold water on it."

The doc had a great sense of humor.

Samson was an islander that loved Marines

Marines love pets, and on Saipan we enjoyed an abundance of them ... a goat, some parrots, at least one water buffalo which as I recall belonged to Charley Rudd, a few cats and the most famous of all, our dog Samson. In spite of the war, some islanders welcomed Marines. Sergeant Bill Kennedy came across a brownish-colored, scroungy-looking, likable mutt carrying a large rock in his mouth. It must have been love at first sight, because the dog followed Kennedy back to our area. He was friendly, as we were, so he stayed. We taught him English and soon changed his eating habits from fish and rice to Spam and potatoes.

Samson readily took to the high moral standards of the 5th Amphtracs. The dog had an affinity for carrying large objects in his mouth. If he could get his jaws around it, no matter how heavy, he would drag it home. Such a peculiar habit was quickly recognized as a valuable asset. Beer rations are highly prized by all servicemen but more so by the Marines. All Navy, Army, Seabees and Airmen camped around us were considered legitimate prey. In some camps, weekly beer rations might amount to a dozen or more cans per man. Much of this was stored between ankles when the owner was seated and engrossed in a poker game; otherwise, the cans were stashed beneath cots for future consumption.

With just a little bit of training, Samson learned to belly-crawl into tents and carefully retrieve unopened cans of beer. We quickly promoted him to requisition officer.

Nearly every night Samson would happily prance into our tent, drop a can and revel in the praise we heaped upon him, topped, of course, with a ration of Spam. Samson would then light out on another foray. If we were lucky, he picked up half a dozen cans a night.

If that mutt could have brought beer back by the case, I'm certain he would have. He was kind of dumb, though. Time and again we had to reprimand him for borrowing from other Marines. When any of our group came to the tent vowing vengeance, we would invite him to sit and talk things over. We pointed out the attributes of this valuable animal and apologized on his behalf, explaining that what he did was for the good of all. The complainant would be reimbursed not only for his loss, but with half a dozen extra cans, at no cost, and sent happily on his way.

Samson shall always be fondly remembered for his total devotion to duty. The other mutts became such nuisances that Doc Hawkins, fearing overpopulation, offered to neuter them. The major and Capt. Stoll thought this a fine idea.

The corpsmen set to work rounding up every dog they could find. Things were going well until about the seventh "fix," when the flap to the operating tent burst open, and in stomped Gunny Sgt. Pierce, flying storm warnings.

"Anyone," he roared, "that would do such a dirty low-down trick on any poor little defenseless animal is a mean, rotten, low-down rat, and nobody is going to do that to my dog ... if I had one!"

Because of Pierce's tirade, Samson was spared the indignity.

Doc Hawkin's Clip Joint

During these halcyon days when there were no battle casualties, fevers, or dogs to fix, Doc Hawkins felt useless. Bullet wounds or the loss of a limb were the only ways to get a Purple Heart out of Hawkins. Shrapnel wounds did not count in his book. With all this quiet he needed something, anything, to occupy his time. There was only one thing left . . . circumcisions!

We often wondered about the doc.

A sign went up at the Med tent; "Clip Joint" Hawkins became known as the Marianas Clipper, instead of the Marianas Dognapper.

A week off duty was the incentive, and many of the boys went for it. I wasn't sure just what the hell a circumcision was, but, when I found out what was going to be cut, I declined.

After the operation, each patient was supplied with a small white apron to wear until healed. Our battalion area was on the heavily traveled main road between Charon Kanoa and Garapan. I don't know what the passing Seabees, Army and Navy guys or the female nurses' thought, but to me it looked as though a bunch of FreeMasons had invaded the camp.

Both our doctors were lieutenants, but somehow a requisition paper appeared; it looked very legitimate, except that Doctor Don Hawkins suddenly became Lt. Commander D. Hanks, C.O. of the 2nd Armored reconnoitering and Hospital Battalion (that title alone should have given someone a clue). His very official looking adjutant was, of course, Major Stanaback. The papers called for a 6x6 truck to be loaded with Navy beer by a Navy work party at the Garapan docks. The requisition was promptly filled. The stern-faced Commander Hanks accepted the salutes, while his adjutant signed the papers. The two then drove off. I suppose the truck was also stolen.

Chapter 12: Teamwork is essential; . . . it gives them other people to shoot at

Hap Ahlgrim and Bill Stoll met with Captain O'Brien, C.O. of the 6th Marines, 2nd Div., then holding the town of Garapan, to discuss using *LVTs* to hold off the enemy infiltration via the offshore reef. After the meeting, the two requested and received, provided they watch out for a Marine patrol in the vicinity, permission to walk through the destroyed town. En route, they wandered through a shelled building with an intact basement loaded with saki, Suntori, whiskey, and Asahi beer (apparently a Japanese officers' club). Without further ado, the two of them dived in.

About that time the patrol appeared. They, too, were thirsty. The patrol leader asked Stoll if he knew they were behind Japanese lines.

"No problem," replied Bill, "there's a patrol way up ahead."

"We are that patrol."

Bill and Hap decided to leave, but not before they helped themselves to several bottles of whiskey.

Back at camp, Hap gave a bottle to Pete Wilgus who, upon reflection, suggested it might be poisoned. Hap didn't think so, because the Japs had left in too much of a hurry. Still, Wilgus wasn't sure. He called Gunny Pierce and offered him a couple of snorts. Pierce left quite happy. Wilgus waited about an hour, then inquired if anyone had seen Pierce and, if so, how was he acting?

Pierce was not happy when he heard of this little plot. Wilgus wasn't happy either when he returned to his tent and found the rest of his whiskey gone. Saki caches back in the hills were gradually being depleted, and whiskey from the airmen was running more than ten dollars a bottle.

There were hillbillies in our outfit who claimed they could make hooch. The moonshiners went to work and soon, as Fred Ehlen observed, "... there were so many stills around camp, if a bomb ever hit one, the resulting explosions would resemble a burning ammo dump."

Eagan figured it would be a good idea if we loaded a green coconut with some raisins and sugar and let it ferment. We carefully cut the top off the biggest coconut we could find and packed it full of the necessary ingredients, sugar, raisins, etc. Then, to bug proof it, we plugged the hole and tightly wrapped the coconut with lots and lots of copper wire. We hung it in the tent, eagerly awaiting the results.

It took less than a week for the inevitable to happen. The copper wire flew like shrapnel. Chunks of putrid coconut and gobs of green slime plastered everything in the tent, which, fortunately, was vacant at the time. It would have been embarrassing explaining fermented coconut wounds. We blamed the explosion on a sniper's bullet.

The reputation of the 5th continued to spread

Our presence on any portion of the island was immediately viewed with suspicion. We resorted to elaborate ruses. A damaged Japanese Phaeton command car was carefully rebuilt and painted appropriately. Official U.S. mail bags, stuffed with newspaper and empty boxes, were stacked in full view on the back seat. The disguise allowed access to every base on the island.

One day, Hap Ahlgrim, Headquarters Co., disappeared. There was no place to go AWOL on the island, so no one was concerned, least of all the grinning Marines who spotted him wearing an Army sergeant's uniform, driving an Army truck and inching slowly along in the Army beer ration line at the depot in Garapan. Hap had traded his .45 pistol for the uniform and a good Samurai sword for the truck. When he got the beer safely back to our camp, he gave a couple cases to our supply sergeant

Teamwork is essential; . . . it gives them other people to shoot at

to report the pistol lost in combat. The sword was later replaced with one from Iwo.

Our unending bounty of beer presented another problem: how to chill it. Our *LVTs* had CO2 fire extinguishers, perfect for the task, but we soon ran out of that supply. Army and Navy had C02 fire extinguishers. Unfortunately, after enough losses, they began guarding them jealously.

Until we could locate refrigerators, we were forced to run over to Isley Field and get the B-24 crews to carry a load of beer up to 20,000 feet where it was very cold. It was well worth the two-case fee. So as not to waste fuel, the airmen would load up with bombs and practice on Rota, a Jap-held island about a hundred miles south. The routine worked great, and everyone was happy, except the Japs, of course. Some of the fellows got a chance to go along. Unfortunately, I never did.

One day, a super weapon, a silver-bellied long-range bomber called a B-29, arrived at Isley. We all went over to see it. It was as big as a freight train. We "ooohed" and "aaahed" and noted it carried as many weapons as an infantry regiment. One of our mathematicians calculated the ship could hold twice as much beer as the 24s, but the new crews wouldn't cooperate. They began to raid Tokyo. Many of us begged rides but were turned down because fuel and weight were critical. In addition to the regular dangers, there was a halfway obstacle coming and going: the Volcano Islands based enemy fighters that inflicted a nasty sting.

Alligator Marines

[A "natural" swimming hole probably the result of a 16 inch shell. After the nurses arrived, we donned trunks for swimming. My butt turned white while the rest of me was a nice brown except for a tinge of yellow caused by the quinine substitute Atabrine]

Chapter 13: How to survive in spite of yourself

Almost everyone in the outfit came down with dengue fever, including me. When patrolling a small mountain named Tipo Pali, suddenly all the strength drained out of me. "Go without me," I told the guys. Not able to regain my strength, I slid down the hillside on my butt to find a road. Barely able to stand, I begged a ride from a passing jeep. The driver delivered me directly to the hospital.

Breakbone fever, another name for dengue, feels like being strapped to a medieval rack, as every bone in your body is slowly broken. You are too weak to even move. Your eyes hurt if open, hurt if closed. On top of that, you hurt if you move and hurt if you don't. Until it runs its course, no relief is possible.

[*With dengue, one doesn't care.*]

They placed my tormented body on a cot in a tent located next to a hundred-foot-high Jap radio tower. One of the tower legs had been shot away. The remaining supports did not look steady. The tower creaked and swayed constantly even in the lightest of island breezes and threatened to fall crushing us all. Let it. With dengue, one doesn't care.

The corpsman suspended a mosquito net over me. That night it rained like hell; a typhoon, rain whistling in horizontally, tent tops boomed like bass drums accompanied by the straining sound of the three-legged tower. Water rose to the top of the cot. I lay soaked. A coconut crab decided to keep dry by crawling up the inside of the net, then horizontally, directly over my face. His weight pulled him down to within an inch of my nose. I awoke to a seashell smell. Eye to eye; maybe to him my nose looked like dinner. I stared deep into the beady eyes of that stupid crab and decided I didn't like this war business.

After a week or so, the fever ran its course and hunger gripped me as well as the others in the tent. The scraps of food we each received daily spooned by a corpsman amounted to a cup of red Jell-O with a slice of peach. Getting to my feet I sneaked into the galley, an oversize tent with stoves, racks and mountains of supplies. Next to the wall of the tent stood an unguarded carrying rack with five covered pots that I presumed contained warm chow. With the cook's attention diverted in the busy galley, I quickly grabbed the rack and manhandled it back to our tent. My prize consisted of three covered pots loaded with pancakes, one pot of syrup and one of butter.

Marshall became the man of the hour.

A 'real' swimming pool

By this time, after all those days of a sweating fever running 104-5 degrees, plus the humidity of the island, a bath was certainly in order. About fifty yards from the hospital area lay a huge, water-filled crater surrounded by several wrecked Japanese airplanes. The hole, about the size of a back yard swimming pool and about the same depth, was probably the result of a 16-inch naval shell.

The water was fresh, the hole filled daily by the abundant rainfall. I jumped in. It was great. I told the others we now had swimming pool. Wow! Jimminy crickets! A real swimming pool!

As each man recovered, he staggered over. We secured a stout plank for a diving board, cleared away a bunch of aircraft wreckage, and then cut some slender poles to make a lanai. It took time, as we were still weak.

We lounged, swam and tanned for about a week. The area became so popular, the earthen sides began to soften and crumble. Each day the pool depth noticeably decreased. Someone hit on the idea of deepening the hole with a couple of grenades. We all agreed. Three grenades were tossed in and exploded one after the other. The concussions not only brought the desired result of deepening the bottom, but also freed two bloated corpses, which bobbed to the surface.

Suddenly we forgave all corpsmen and all doctors for inflicting those godawful, arm-numbing shots we suffered in boot camp and aboard the Sea Witch. Now we fervently hoped they hadn't overlooked any.

Everyone considered himself lucky, because the worst we got was a severe case of ringworm.

Another moneymaking scheme down the drain

On my release from the canvas hospital, I returned to our hovel only to find Ege had moved us to a fine Jap dugout down on Red Beach. We returned to the swimming hole area, not to swim, but to carve aluminum from the wrecked Jap planes. We discovered that the point of the knife blade in our mess kit gear, if rocked properly, would make nice engraving marks on the soft metal.

We proceeded to produce engraved watchbands and bracelets by the dozens. The tropical scenes, palms, mountains and clouds we carved looked very professional. The Navy guys, our best customers, bought them at two dollars apiece. Fortunately for us, most of the swabbies shipped out before they discovered that Japanese aluminum against the skin caused a severe rash. Not all of the metal had that effect, but we still had to give back the dough to the men who hadn't yet left the island. Another moneymaking scheme down the drain.

Our guys were always ingenious for grand ideas, and our motor pool men were the best. Saipan had a tiny narrow-gage railroad with a peanut whistle type engine. Though the engine was shell damaged, our mechanics got it operating. The tracks ran almost all around the island. We got together some small flatcars and figured we could sell excursions. This idea fizzled when we discovered that the heavy 6x6 trucks bent the light-gauge tracks wherever there was a crossing.

A parade ground?

Eventually, after we moved to a more permanent camp area across the road from Red Beach, our officers insisted we needed a parade ground. A parade ground? 5th Amphs had never paraded as a unit. Why start now? At this late stage, it was highly doubtful that anyone could keep step.

Parade grounds meant inspections and stuff. This would cause a great inconvenience to our personal liberty.

The decision had been made, and there was no getting around it. Had we been prisoners of war, which in effect we were, we could not have worked any slower. Shovels broke, wheelbarrows collapsed, and the weather was too hot or too rainy. Some new *LVT-4s* arrived, and one was divested of its loading ramp, which was dragged around by another tractor to level the designated area. If the tractors were spun just right, the growsers gouged large ditches in the earth. Unless the ramp was weighted, the scraper would skim right over these ditches. Several men were ordered to provide the weight. That worked until "Tank" Miller, heaviest man in the outfit, fell off the scraper and broke his leg. Construction temporarily stopped, which was fine by us.

Still, our officers persisted. A better solution had to be found. Our mechanics were assigned the job. They took an old Jap tank and removed gun and turret, along with other unnecessary junk. I helped. It was interesting to note that a small metal cup placed to drain oil into the bearing cavity lubricated the bearings on the Jap tank. It was a spring-actuated cap that closed and prevented dirt from entering. Atop that cap were imprinted the words, "Gits Bros. Mfg.Co Chicago, 111." It just so happened that Remi Gits, millionaire inventor of that oil cup, was my uncle, married to my mother's sister, Tillie.

The mechanics welded a tow bar to the rear of the tank and devised a passable scraper that could be weighted with sand bags instead of beer-guzzling Marines. In no time at All, they leveled the area and we had ... a baseball diamond! A surprise from our brass. The men immediately formed teams and issued challenges to any and all units on the island.

Sometimes life was not as rosy as one would like. On at least one occasion a couple of our officers took exception to some act committed, intentionally or not, by our C.O.. The two voiced their extreme displeasure by the mounting of a machine gun in a hidden gully and proceeded to stitch the top of the major's tropical villa with .30-caliber ball, A.P. and tracer. The major didn't care for this. After shooting off much of the roof, they hustled the weapon to another location and strolled back into the area whistling innocently.

Lieutenants Joe Reese and Spike Malcolm investigated the incident but came up with no suspects. They did, however, voice extreme concern over the dangers of renegade Japanese still hiding in the mountains.

There were other methods of showing displeasure. Once, during a weapons inspection, a round, accidentally triggered, of course, sang harmlessly over inspecting officer Capt. Stoll's head. I believe that was the last inspection we ever had.

[*Rescuing the orphans*[

Chapter 14: You will enjoy recreation, whether you like it or not

The Pacific war raged on. Guam was retaken. 1st, 6th and 8th Amphtrac Btns. crossed the reefs of Peleliu with heavy losses. Elements of the 10th Amphs landed on Leyte. The Army and the Navy were punching the hell out of the Japanese fleet.

Yet, life on Saipan was rather idyllic. Much time was found for recreation. Some outfits staged boxing matches. Stoll, having considerable boxing experience, approached Hap to represent the battalion. Hap, overly confident with this singular honor, immediately challenged a much-touted heavyweight, said to be the champ of the island. Bill voiced his misgivings; not only was Hap over 30, but he was out of training. Hap was adamant.

In front of some 200 spectators, Hap hit the deck twice in the first round. Bill became nervous, but Ahlgrim assured him all was okay.

"Relax," he said, "I'm the one taking the shots and I can take care of myself."

In the second round, Hap took two more trips to the canvas. Stoll wanted to throw in the towel.

"I'll never forgive you if you do," growled the boxer.

Down again in the third round. Again, he refused to stop. Hap championed the 5th Amphs by staying the entire ten rounds. That's the kind of guy he was, but his boxing days were over.

'Keep up the morale of the troops' became the catchphrase. Units all over the island organized softball teams. Ours was coached by our own C.0., Major Shead.

Who would be the Island champs?

The island champs would earn unrestricted access to a large walk-in refrigerator filled with beer. That coveted position became the topic of conversation for weeks. To insure its integrity, the reefer unit was surrounded by a welded iron cage, wrapped in heavy tow chains and padlocked. On the day of the big game, the staff NCO team, representing the honor of the 5th Amphs, showed up so drunk it was thought they couldn't play. Nevertheless, valiant Alligator men that they were, the game started on time. The score was 21-0 in the first inning, not in our favor. The game was called when a fly ball to the forehead cold-cocked our company gunny, Irv Rogers. We lost. The victors jubilantly cut away the iron restraints on the reefer, only to find it empty.

There were those who suspected the NCOs. But there were no real clues.

Entertainment island style

An outdoor movie screen was set up near Charon Kanoa, sand bag seats and everything. Price of admission was to come armed. Japs, you know. A poncho was a good idea, too; it usually rained. Lizards enjoyed scampering over the screen, catching bugs attracted by the light. The screen was transparent, the movie could be enjoyed from both sides.

The Japs quickly took advantage of this. If they didn't like the feature, they threw stones, coconuts or, sometimes, grenades. One evening we prepared a .30 machine gun and waited. At the first sound of rustling in the foliage, the boys cut loose. In the morning, looking for our kill, we found a dead water buffalo. Well, it made a great barbecue!

The cowboys in our outfit decided it was time for a real, down home rodeo. Charley Willoughby was one, and, I think, Dale Romans, Onnie Harbison, Centifonto, Charley Rudd and Ed Powers got into the act. They wanted to start the event with a horse race but could not find any horses anywhere. Water buffaloes would have to do. A track was laid out and the event advertised. Bettors arrived from all over the island.

[*Saipan Caribou*]

The animals were eyeballed and bets were laid. Through the *Stars and Stripes* newspaper, we learned that the British had nicknamed our tractors "Buffaloes." We were thus considered experts in the field of animal husbandry. I would imagine, had we raced live alligators, the reasoning would have been the same. The 5th supplied bookmakers, beer booths and a Las Vegas type crap table.

One of the animals had gaping shrapnel wound across its tail. When the tail would swing in one direction, the wound would open, allowing an invasion of swarming flies. On the return swing, the slower flies were trapped in the closing maw. Other than that, the beasts appeared in good condition.

A pistol shot and the race was on! Charley, aboard Fairy Maiden, lumbered away from the gate, while competitor Daisy Mae, jockeyed by Romans, had a bit of difficulty deciding which direction was best. Around the far turn, both barechested, sweating jockeys, exhorting the utmost from the gallant steeds, raced neck and neck. Suddenly, Fairy Maiden bumbled to the lead .... No, Daisy Mae is now in front! Oh, ladies and gentlemen, what a race . . . .! Now they are neck and neck coming down the home stretch ... it appears as though . . . wait a minute, something has occurred . . . Daisy Mae is faltering, she is rolling over . . . Daisy Mae is dead!

A fair win? You bet, said some. No way, said others. The fight was on.

When things calmed down, the crap table opened, financed by some boys from "A" and "B" companies. For safety's sake, they printed and sold script. Brilliant idea, but someone found out and immediately duplicated hundreds of dollars' worth. To top off everything else, the first shooter threw seven passes in a row. The table wen bankrupt.

We fooled Eleanor Roosevelt

I continued honing my jungle skills, preparing for the inevitable approaching action. I had seen the movie *King Kong* and knew almost every island in the Pacific had a high, cloud-encased mountain in the center with a strong possibility of dinosaurs, similar to the lizard I had encountered earlier. On the other side of the coin, all the islands without mountains were beautiful sandy atolls, teeming with swaying palms and sarong-clad Dorothy Lamours.

Somehow the horror shown in photos of Guadalcanal and Tarawa escaped me. I ignored the reality here on Saipan. After all, I was bulletproof and loved the smell of cordite.

Every spare moment found me harassing the Japanese in the hills. Sometimes others in the 5th, Walt Physter, Aaron Riddle and Charlie Rudd, would accompany Ege and me. Sometimes I went alone. For whatever reason, all details of my first encounter with a live Japanese soldier have been erased from my mind. I only remember he was an older man and had a rather gentle, fatherly face.

I killed him anyway.

On another occasion, Bob Hoover, Marcus Gutierrez, Dale Romans, and probably Chuck Schindler and I discovered a starving old woman hiding near Marpi Point. The poor soul was dirty, frightened and probably someone's grandmother. We brought her back to the civilian compound where she was kindly treated, cleaned up and fed. She thought she would be raped and killed. We fooled her *and* Eleanor Roosevelt. According to the first lady and certain women's groups, such Marine savagery was normal. They advocated that Marines returning to the states should be isolated on some remote island and go through a period of humanizing before being allowed to enter the mainstream of civilized life. We could take that insult, but when she and they proposed stopping our beer supply, that was going too damned far! The uproar was tremendous . . . the idea was dropped.

I often wonder if the little ones survived

On one of our forays behind Marpi Point airfield, Ege and I came across four starving, almost naked children, three little girls, and a small boy. Their arms and legs were thin as sticks, their bellies swollen. Hungry flies edged their eyes. Their matted hair was covered with filth. They had been abandoned amid death and destruction and now were at the mercy of two ugly Alligator Marines.

We could not leave them. We put them between us on the trail. I was point; Eagan brought up the rear. The older girl, around six or seven, weak as she was, attempted to carry the sick little boy on her back. She staggered and fell. She began sobbing, apparently afraid we would leave or kill him. I had half a candy bar in my pocket and divided it among them. Ege had a bit of water left, which the four gratefully drank.

They brightened a bit. Ege tried to carry the little boy but failed, as he was coming down with dengue. Now we were in a fix, and our progress slowed considerably. We came upon a small, devastated hamlet with several ruined buildings and many bodies, both civilian and military. Possibly even the parents of the little ones were among them.

The ground was littered with fallen roofs and walls, smashed and burned furniture, hundreds of heavy, green glass saki bottles abuzz with thousands of flies.

Looking around for some type of wagon, I found a low handcart with bicycle-style wheels. At the same time I discovered a Jap soldier trying to conceal himself beneath a fallen wall. I intended to shoot him but, instead, motioned him out and back to our little group. I placed the kids on the cart, covered them against the broiling sun with large banana leaves and, in sign language, ordered my prisoner to pull the cart. He refused. I persuaded him with the aid of a stick the size of a baseball bat. He appreciated it when I gave him some of what little water I had left.

Progress remained slow but easier. Poor Ege was doing all he could to just keep up. It took almost all day to cover the six miles to Tanapag. We halted many times. The little ones were in bad shape. As sick as he was, Eagan tried to bathe their heads with a damp rag, but it soon dried up. During our rests, I kept close watch on the prisoner. We began to converse in sign language. He wasn't a bad guy. He knew the word "whiskey" and I knew the word "saki;" we laughed. He was nineteen, by finger count, and seemed surprised and mortified that I was only seventeen.

An Army truck drove by. I requested that the soldiers take the tykes to the compound and our prisoner to the POW camp. They agreed and probably took credit for the capture and rescue. I got a jeep and took my buddy to the hospital. He recovered in a couple of weeks.

I often wonder if the little ones survived and how they are today. The soldier lived only because he put his pride aside and pulled that cart. I don't know if he realized that.

Chapter 15: Professionals are predictable but the world is full of amateurs

Still burning from not taking part in the initial invasion, Eagan and I were not going to miss out on the complete capture of the Marianas. A very small island, Aquijan, lay just to the southwest about 2 miles off Tinian. It might have contained a radio station in contact with the Jap military on some other island, but it posed no threat.

The two of us decided to capture it or, at least, shoot up the place and then run like hell. We packed our outrigger with rifles, grenades, beer and other necessities for our foray. Just before our planned departure, we heard rumors that our battalion was going to invade Aguijan just for practice. Time was of the essence to beat them to it.

Somebody got wind of our intentions and casually mentioned that the place was a leper colony. We changed our minds, unloaded the canoe, sat on the beach and drank the beer.

A few days later, Capt. Bill Clark, Plans and Training officer, was ordered to work up the logistics on taking the island using "C" Company men and tractors only, to give "A" and "B" companies a needed break. Working with Lt. Col. John Griebal, plans were drawn for a 2nd Div. rifle company, under Major Haffner, a Shore Fire Control party from the Navy and a group of observers for Air Liaison to head up the initial strike with a battalion of 8th Marines held in reserve. Ege and I opted not to mention that it was a leper colony. It would be a great joke to let Clark find out for himself.

Beginning the 23rd of August, surface bombardment and air strikes worked over the island for three days. Aguijan was terraced with steep cliffs all around. Aerial photos indicated only one possible landing place, a small concrete ramp used for unloading supply boats. Capt. Clark reserved a Patrol Craft from the navy, then, accompanied by a party of Marine officers, set out to reconnoiter the place. It was a boring trip. On arrival, the *PC* circled the objective several times. There was no activity; apparently the artillery and strafing had done a good job. Everyone lounged on deck, joking and drinking coffee. The operation would be a snap. Just for the fun of it, the Navy crew opened up with their small guns, firing on any target they could spot, which consisted mainly of a few ruined houses and small caves.

Everything was going just fine. Several splashes were observed around the boat. The gunners explained that they were caused by bits of wadding from the deck guns. Then, a strange ka-chunk, ka-chunk indicated something was striking the vessel, followed by the chilling whine of 20mm and other small-caliber missiles sailing past the ears of the coffee drinkers.

Suddenly, smoke billowed from the stern of the boat, where all the depth charges were racked. The Navy ran for fire hoses, while the Marines ran for life jackets. There were eight deadly charges on board, the detonation of any one of which could blow the vessel in half. The Damage Control party hosed the rear half of the boat and squelched the smoke.

When things calmed down, it was discovered that a Jap slug had ignited a smoke screen pot near the explosives. The chagrined skipper, fearing a fire, ordered the depth charges jettisoned as the boat beat a hasty retreat toward Saipan. The humiliated crewmen dutifully rolled each bomb off the stern but forgot to put the charges on safe. One by one, they sank to the depths and exploded . . . giving the *PC* some terrific impetus along the way.

In the mean time, someone noticed a crew member missing. The boat circled vainly numerous times. Finally, with heavy hearts, all agreed the man was lost, only to discover, on their return, that the sailor, suffering from a hangover, had fallen over the side on the way out from Garapan. He swam to shore, caught a truck back to the slopchute and continued his binge.

With the misadventures of the recon officers and the *PC* boat, the officers decided to forget the miniature invasion. Our "leper colony" joke on Bill fell flat, and the Japs lived in peace until July of 1945, when another company of Marines captured the tiny island.

Gas mask class

Gas masks were a real pain to carry; yet the threat of poison gas was always present. Our gas officer, Lt. Waldo Wilson, assigned me the task of training men to recognize odors of the type of gas expected.

A tightly closed tent lined with benches was our classroom. It was always 200 degrees inside. My job was to explain how gas might be delivered, where it would accumulate and possible treatment. At the end of each lecture, I demonstrated by breaking a small vial of 5% solution of mustard or chlorine gas, just to familiarize the men with the odor. Even with that small amount, several times I got sloppy and wound up blistered. Then, just for the fun of it, I ordered everyone to don and test their gas masks while I ignited a paper impregnated with tear gas crystals. When the gas cloud had filled the tent, I ordered everyone to remove his mask. The effect was remarkable . . . everyone raced, teary eyed, for the outside. I thought it a novel way to dismiss class, but did not make friends.

Hole in the Wall gang

Shortly thereafter, the unexpected happened. They promoted me to corporal. I was proud and thought back to Camp Pendleton and to what Lt. Williams had told me, "Kid, you'll make a Marine yet."

Months earlier, when we slogged ashore, we naturally asked if there were any way to make money on the island. We were informed that a Marine had blown a safe he found in the sugar mill and had taken out $20,000. What the hell, we believed it. As it turned out, it didn't happen in the sugar mill and there was no 20 grand, but, naturally, some of our guys were involved. I was told a patrol unit— Capt. Stoll, Gus Paris and a couple of others— found a locked safe in a ruined building in the once-picturesque town of Garapan. Their eyes immediately filled with visions of gold, jewels and other exotic Oriental riches. Hastily, they wired the iron box with explosives. Being amateurs in the finer art of safe cracking, the charge brought down the remaining ceiling and walls. It not only failed to open the safe but topped it face down on its own door.

A squad of MPs arrived. Our people, looking as innocent as possible, blamed the noise on a booby trap. After the MPs departed, the would-be *Hole in the Wall* gang muscled the safe onto its back. Another charge proved more successful. The booty consisted of one American quarter, nothing else.

Chapter 16: Try to look unimportant; they may be low on ammo

The cry of "Condition Red," accompanied by the wailing, hand-cranked device we called a "sighreen," because it would "sigh" before it would "reen," alerted us to anything from a possible Japanese naval task force just off shore to Banzai suicide paratroopers climbing down the chimney. Of course, none of these perils materialized, but we did come under constant day and night air raids. We had two alerts in July for possible attack from naval forces. We wondered if they'd come ashore in their clumsy small, ineffective land tanks fitted with large, ungainly pontoons or landing barges similar to our Higgins boats. It was a wait-and-see situation that never developed.

Air raids kept us pretty much on the move. During the month of August, '44, we had raids on the 12th, 15th and 19th. In September we had only one or two. Usually the planes came in low and headed directly for Isley (Aslito) airfield to strafe the bombers. They'd make two or three passes, drop bombs, then swing over our area and give us hell.

On September 30th, our ammo dump, located next to our tent area, blew up. As is usual with ammo fires, shot and shell screamed in every direction. My idiot pal and I sat in the company street watching the fireworks, while everyone else headed for safety. We watched our tents get peppered and thought it funny as all get-out until a mortar round landed near enough to part our hair. Then we ran, too.

The crime of getting caught

Sam Nuzzo was pulling guard duty on a six-man prisoner work detail. They were all from the 5th, and this group represented one of the only times our people were ever caught acquiring property belonging to someone else. The prisoners alleged crime was stealing sick bay alcohol, though the bigger crime was that of getting caught.

While guarding the so-called prisoners, an air raid alarm sounded, "... brave as I was," said Sam later, "... I warned the prisoners to take cover, then I took off running and jumped in the nearest hole. All my prisoners followed me. They, of course, landed on top of me . . . all six of 'em. I think they injured me, but I never got a medal for my act of bravery."

Shrapnel rain

November 2nd was the first of a full week of raids, and on the 26th and 27th we had several daylight raids, which were very interesting. We could watch the show.

On December 5th, a P-38 shot down a high-altitude bomber. Someone said two Japs bailed out, but I didn't see them.

When the alarm sounded, we headed for the slit trenches as fast as we could, but it was boring sitting out there all night in the rain. Later we more or less took our time. Crouching in the open trenches was not the safest place. Tracers crisscrossed the night sky while, thousands of feet above, ack-ack flashes bounced off the stars. All of this action threw thousands of pounds of metal into the sky, which eventually rained down.

We quickly learned to anticipate the arrival of falling steel by the sound. It started with a low hum that gradually grew in intensity. At its loudest, hot pieces of jagged metal began clanging off tractors, ripping through our tents and our more valuable possessions, slashing our backs and arms as we crouched in the trenches. Most of this deadly shrapnel rain came from our own gunfire tearing things up. Occasionally, before my size 15 boots arrived, I would step barefoot on a hot piece and, amid much laughter from the trenches, shoot about ten feet in the air.

False alarms were not uncommon. There were times when happy gunners fired on our own planes. I once watched a cargo

Try to look unimportant; they may be low on ammo

plane from another island get plastered. I don't know if any of our pilots were killed or injured, but I imagine the survivors spit out a few choice words.

After a while, many of us casually sauntered to the trenches. We departed the tents with a minimum of clothing, a maximum of beer, cigarettes and a poncho to cover us when we smoked. We perched on the edge of the trench and watched the bombs hit Isley field a mile to the south. Knowing the dumb Japs couldn't do anything right, we developed a "laissez-faire" attitude. As usual, we were soon to be proved wrong.

The first of the B-29s left for Tokyo on November 24, '44. Eighty of them filled the sky. Those slant-eyes were going to catch hell now. Not all was as rosy as we thought; maybe there was a radio on Aguijan (the supposed leper island) broadcasting the bombers departure to Tokyo and islands to the north.

In a chain of islands known as the Nanpo Shoto, halfway between Saipan and Japan, the southernmost of the group was known as Iwo Jima. It contained two operating airfields with a third under construction. From here came the raiders that hit us so often on Saipan, a mere 625 miles to the south, and from here rose the deadly fighters to harass our B-29s that must fly directly over the island to and from the Japanese mainland.

On the 27th, two newer Mitsubishi Ki-67 bombers came in low over our area and slammed Isley field hard—one B-29 totaled, eleven seriously damaged. The raiders flew back in triumph. Tadamichi Kuribayashi, commander of that hot volcanic speck, figured it would be wiser to destroy the silver monsters on the ground than in the air. He immediately ordered a return mission. Again, we were caught flatfooted. Three more of the giant planes went up in smoke. There were a number of casualties.

Our careless air raid habits began to change. Some of the fellows started sleeping in their clothes; others kept helmet, dungarees and shoes in easily accessible places and grabbed them on the run. One night came the inevitable.

The bombers were upon us before the raucous wail of the sighreen pierced the soft, perfumed tropical air. The Kis,[1] called Bettys, charged in again under our radar. No grace period. No warning. Everyone scrambled for cover from exploding bombs and burning targets.

My "easily accessible clothing" got kicked all over in the rush. I managed to snatch my shorts and tried to pull them on while running. I was barefoot *again* and the last to evacuate the tent. A thermite flare burst overhead; our whole area was awash in bright light. I saw the approach of a twin-engine bomber flanked by fighters[2] at each wing tip. They flew at treetop level, about 20 feet. Flame spouted from the bomber's tail. I rejoiced that our gunners had hit something.

I stood in awe, barefoot, my mouth open, one hand holding up my unbuttoned shorts. Then it dawned on me that what I thought were flames was actually sweeping muzzle flashes from the plane's rear 12.7mm guns.

To this day, I can clearly see the man's goggled face. He looked down at me and grinned. He swung those twins and began stitching the ground toward me. Everything was happening in slow motion! Sand leap up, each spurt coming closer as I ran. My legs pumped up and down as if they were in glue; I felt the sting of the erupting sand and the shock waves from the slugs. I dove for a trench, landing heavily atop the crouched occupants. It was a close call. Unfortunately, a 2nd Armored man, Corp. John Bistline, caught some of those slugs and was killed.

The marauder veered left over the water and made another run toward the airfield. When just over the civilian compound, our gunners nailed it. I clambered off my buddies and accepted

---

[1] The Ki-67 Mitsubishi was a 334-mph Japanese bomber comparable with the twin-engine light bombers then in use by other major combatants. For an aircraft of its size, its maneuverability was outstanding.

[2] Probably the excellent, long-range fighter/bomber, Nakajima Ki-84.

their congratulations on my narrow escape. Emory Prine, Charley Rudd and Dale Romans brushed themselves off, nursed some bruises and proceeded to berate me, "Dammit, Marshall, when you landed on us we thought we got hit by a five hundred pound dud!"

The whole outfit agreed.

First and foremost, a rifleman

Air raids on December 19, 23, and 25, inflicted more damage to the airfield and planes. On the 27th, we had two raids. At the same time, five infiltrators sneaked into our tractor area. Three were killed on the beach; two escaped. I don't know who shot the three, I didn't, even though everyone gave me the credit. There were more raids, one on the 2nd of January and one on the 5th. I think those were the last.

A Marine is, first and foremost, a rifleman. So as not to lose sight of this concept, a rifle range was constructed back in the hills. The range soon presented us with two unexpected problems.

The flour paste used to seal holes in the paper targets was being used up at an unprecedented rate. It wasn't that we were such good shots; our cooks claimed we were just sloppy. They were tired of being constantly beseeched to mix more and more paste.

The mystery was finally cleared with the discovery of split-toed tracks in the soft mud. The Japanese had been stealing the paste for their miso soup!

The M-1 Garand was a powerful and excellent weapon. I preferred it to the smaller, more mobile carbine used by most other Marines. Still, there were Marines who adored the much older Springfield '03 bolt action rifle. The "old breed" would go to almost any lengths to obtain one, especially Lt. Spike Malcolm. One day, while at the range and happily banging away with his '03, Spike was spotted by General T. E. Watson, a genuine "old breed" who came up through the ranks, a mustang.

"What the hell is that man doing with second Division property?" he roared.

Spike was a 90-day officer and still slightly awed by the presence of a general. Before he could sputter an answer, the short-tempered Watson went into a tirade about the 5th Amphtracs and their propensity toward acquiring other people's property. Another officer, General R. Hunt, managed to calm Watson after Capt. Stoll explained that many weapons were retrieved from the bottom of the lagoon at the landing beach by divers Eagan and Marshall. And the 5th amphibious Tractor Battalion, like all good Marines, take good care of equipment and recondition all recovered items for future use.

It was a perfectly logical explanation with which the good general could not argue. Nevertheless, a few days later an order came through that all 5th Amphtrac weapons were to be inventoried and any unauthorized arms surrendered.

There went about half our arsenal.

Chapter 17: Leaving Paradise

Saipan was becoming overpopulated. Newly constructed buildings emerged at an alarming rate. A regular highway ran the complete length of the island from Nafutan Point to northern Marpi Point and back again along the far side of the island.

Second and 4th Division cemeteries, though beautiful and well tended, instilled a serene sadness. We would soon be leaving, but friends like Rudy Chaves, Emmett Altizer, Norv Green, Ikenberry and many others were staying. I avoided visiting them. I did not want to say goodbye. In spite of imagined shortcoming, 5th Amphs was a sharp outfit composed of good, clean cut American men trained to kill, steal, beg or connive to gain the upper edge. Under the watchful eyes of our officers, training continued with a vengeance.

[*The Paradise we were leaving...*]

We plowed into the ocean for hours and days, driving, radio operating, backing onto and driving off rolling *LSTs*. We followed compass directions for hours across the broiling, trackless ocean, bobbing and puking to the constant roar of the huge, seven-cylinder 250 horsepower Continental engine and its eternal pall of carbon monoxide fumes. The armor would get too hot to touch; we prayed for a breeze to create a wave that would splash through the open hatch for a moment's relief. Then, when that did happen, we'd be blinded by steam from the hot transmission and curse the stinging salt crust left behind. Nevertheless, we were damned good Marines and proud of it.

Multi-colored tractors for Iwo Jima

Though being barefoot, having lost my boots in that harrowing night raid, brought me no discomfort, I feared I might be left out of the next operation. Bowing to some pressure from somewhere, our company C.O., Charles Schultz, placed me on light duty. Time hung heavy, and I begged for something to do. Our tractors, all painted a dull green, were being spruced up for a pre-action inspection by some general in the 4th Div. Our *LVT-4s* were properly aligned on the beach facing the road. Each vehicle was covered with a canvas tightly tied over cab and cargo area. In spite of this protection, constant tropical dampness created rampant, ugly rust stains that ran down from the bolts and clamps holding the light armor in place. To keep me occupied and out of trouble, Malcolm suggested I paint out these unsightly rust streaks running down each tractor.

I trotted happily off to Supply for brush and paint. Unfortunately, Supply had no paint, all having been used for the coming inspection.

"Try 2nd Armor. They might have some."

They, too, were out of paint and suggested I might find some at 7th Field Depot. It was just my luck . . . *every bit of green paint* on the island had already been used. The only paint

Leaving Paradise

available was a light grey-blue paint used by the Navy. Determined to get rid of those stains, this did not hamper me. I had a job to do and, by golly, I was going to do it. Grey-blue paint it was.

On about my fourth or fifth tractor, Schultz came by and promptly had a kitten— so did Shead— when he saw my creations. Every single rust streak was duly painted, leaving each tractor beautifully striped, sort of like a herd of African zebras, only, instead of black and white, they were light blue over drab jungle green.

"What the hell happened?" yelled Reece. "Who is the moron that did that?"

My chest puffed up, I saluted and answered, "In the absence of the proper color paint, and with the liability of rusting equipment, the inspecting officer should be reassured by my efforts to preserve our few resources."

"Nuts," he said.

For some reason, all our brass became very excited. Inspection was the following day and zebra tractors would not pass muster.

A hurried call to Naval Intelligence explained the problem, and Schultz inquired as to whether this light grey-blue color would have any negative effect on the upcoming operation.

The first response brought the usual, "Who was the moron who did that?"

Naval Intelligence said they would check and get back to him. They did. Supreme command returned the call. Our red-faced officers' explanations were that the 5th Amphs, unfortunately, were saddled with a barefoot idiot who probably was in league with the Japanese.

Supreme Command thought it over and suggested, in the absence of jungle green and, in the interest of uniformity, all the newly striped tractors be repainted in a uniform Navy grey-blue and the 5th Amphs would answer for it later.

They made me work through the night.

For inspection the tractors were perfectly aligned, all dull green except for several grey/blue "C" company tractors at the far end of the row. Someone diverted the inspecting general to the officers' club just before he got to that end of the line.

The problem eased somewhat when a call from Naval Intelligence informed all concerned that camouflage paint on tractors was of no consequence whatsoever since no trees, rocks or anything else offered protection or concealment at the intended landing site.

Hell, *I* knew that ....

It was then that I painted a mermaid on the side of my machine to celebrate the arrival of my new boots.

The following week, our multi-colored tractors roared shoreward in the first waves on a tiny volcanic island called Iwo Jima.]

Chapter 18: A band of brothers

Through brilliant strategy, precise planning, and total commitment to a cause already lost, a tenacious Samurai warrior converted a less than eight-square-mile piece of rock into an almost impregnable stone fortress. Iwo Jima, a miserable dot in the vast Pacific, mid-way between Saipan and Tokyo, and its doomed but gallant garrison was destined to stand alone in a vicious thirty-six-day battle against the largest Navy/Marine operation ever assembled in the history of mankind.

America's combined force of eight battleships, twelve escort carriers, nineteen cruisers and forty-four destroyers pounded this flyspeck island with thousands of tons of high explosives. Behind the formidable force of warships lay forty-three transports crammed with fighting Marines, Navy, and Army personnel. The entire armada consisted of 800 ships and almost a quarter of a million men poised to attack Iwo first and then proceed to Okinawa.

The Nanpo Shoto islands, now considered a military doorway to Japan, had been ignored for years.[1] First charted in 1543 by Bernard de Torres, they were considered valueless.

In 1673, an Englishman dismissed the southernmost island with a singular comment, "...it had a vile smell, like sulfur".

The Russians didn't want the islands either, particularly Iwo. It lacked water and animal life, sustained little flora and, except for sulfur, contained no minerals.

---

[1]

A small group of mountainous islands, variously known as Ogasawara Shoto, the Bonins (a corruption of <u>bunin</u>, meaning uninhabited) and Volcano Islands. The Japanese believe the islands were first discovered by Ogasawara Sadayori in 1593 and officially surveyed by the Tokugawa shogunate in 1675. Two of the 30 islands, Chichi (Father) Jima and Haha (Mother) Jima are now Japan's smallest national park. Though Io or Iwo Jima still maintains an air base, the island is considered a national shrine.

Commodore Matthew Perry suggested in 1853 that one of the islands might be utilized for a coaling station, but the U.S. rejected that idea.

A few white people settled on Chichi Jima in 1827, and, up until WW II, the descendants of Nathaniel Savory, a Massachusetts whaleman, celebrated the Fourth of July by flying the American flag.

Nobody cared when Japan picked up ownership of the islands in 1861. Haha Jima and Chichi Jima were marginally suited for habitation, but Iwo Jima to the south, half-way between the Marianas and the Japanese mainland, was not only more obscure; it was almost obscene. It was merely a poor suburb of Tokyo, an isolated outpost that exported sulfur and a bit of sugar cane. A thousand or so civilians worked the sulfur pits, grew sugar cane and tended small gardens. Several small hamlets, Higashi (east), Nishi (west), Kita (north), and Minami (south) surrounded the main village of Motoyama.

Motoyama included a store, an inn, a school, some government offices and a geisha house. Motoyama (high place for community garden) was hardly the metropolis its name implies. It was perched over a live volcano; the ground was always hot. About fifty small homes dotted the area. Each building's gutters piped precious rainwater to central cisterns.

Communication with the mainland was sporadic via a supply vessel every two or three months, maybe. The only favorable landing spot was the East Boat Basin. Here, in 1937, the Japanese posted a sign against trespassing [2] as if anyone cared to. Chidori's number 1 airfield was constructed in 1940.

---

[2] Printed in Japanese and English, "Trespassing, surveying, photographing, sketching, modeling, etc., upon these premises without previous official permission are prohibited by the Military Secrets Law. Any offender in this regard will be punished with the full extent of the law."

A band of brothers

In 1944, by personal order of the emperor, Lieutenant-General Tadamichi Kuribayashi was posted to this isolated speck and told to hold the island regardless of the cost.

That, he vowed he would do. "May my ancestors guide me."

The last line of defense for Japan

Kuribayashi had spent 30 of his 54 years in the Army. His duty stations, in addition to military schools in Japan, included embassies in the United States and Canada. He was fluent in English and studied cavalry tactics at Fort Bliss, Texas. He commanded a cavalry regiment in combat in the early '30s in the Japanese sweep through Manchuria and then a brigade in northern China. Later, he served as chief of staff of the Twenty-third Army during the capture of Hong Kong. Though he loved and admired America, he was a true Japanese patriot, a direct descendant of the Samurai. Five generations of his ancestors served six different emperors. His most recent military assignment had been the command of the Imperial Palace Guard. Before departing to this outpost, Kuribayashi received the singular honor of a personal audience with Emperor Hirohito.

The general was not favorably impressed when he arrived at Iwo. The airfield was inadequate and incomplete; defenses were miserable. Bickering between the Navy Command, Captain Tsunezo Wachi and Colonel Kanehiko Atsuchi of the Army prevented any progress in building Iwo's fortifications. Rear Admiral Teiichi Matsunaga and his airmen remained aloof and offered no assistance to either side.

Kuribayashi was appalled to learn that Lt. General Eiryo Obata, commander of the 31st Army on Saipan, ordered the artillery on Iwo's northern high ground moved to the beaches, despite the fact that such beach defenses failed in every instance of an American landing. He angrily countermanded Obata's order. The heavy guns were laboriously hauled back to the hills or concealed at the base of Suribachi. It was the general's first order and not well received.

He was proven correct with the fall of Saipan and again, later, with Obata's death on Tinian, but now, he needed more of everything. Accompanied by his new aide, Major Yoshitaka Horie, a veteran severely wounded by machine gun fire in China, the two paced off nearly every foot of the less-than-five-mile-long island.

They stood atop the dormant Suribachi and noted the 800-yard-wide neck of land connecting this mountain with the lower volcano to the north, the site of Motoyama village. Between the two points lay Chidori airfields 1 and 2. The second field was constructed in 1943. The men figured there might be enough room for a third field just beyond the village.

Haste was paramount. Nearby American Naval task groups' 58.1 and 58.4 fighters swooped in and destroyed 7 planes on the ground and blew 10 out of the air. They returned the following day to blast another 63 planes on the ground. Matsunaga, whose 22nd bomber group destroyed the British battleships *Prince of Wales* and *Repulse* two years before, sent fighters to meet the Americans and to reinforce the beleaguered airmen at Saipan. Admiral Joe Clark's pilots met the squadron halfway. The Japanese lost 66 planes.

Two months prior to the American invasion of Iwo, Matsunaga and his decimated flyers returned to Japan.

Kuribayashi knew, if this last line of defense fell, Japan would soon follow. Construction on gun emplacements and another airfield began immediately, along with a system of underground fortifications and facilities designed to hold an entire army. He clamored for, and got, some of Japan's best soldiers, the 145th Infantry Regiment from Kagoshima, followed by the 2nd Mixed Brigade of 5000 men formerly stationed at Chichi Jima.

At the end of June, the Japanese created the III Air Fleet at Kisarazu and brought the forces at Iwo Jima under the command of the XXVII Air Wing. Loads of cement, rebar, ammunition, foodstuffs, fuel and weapons, troops and experienced miners were ferried in by any means possible, by planes, fishing boats, even sampans. Though U.S. subs continued to take a terrific toll on regular shipping, the general was getting nearly everything he wanted. Now came some house cleaning. He ordered civilians and dissenting officers shipped out. He had no time for either.

Appointed chief of staff of the 109th Division, Colonel Takaishi succeeded Colonel Shizuichi Horie, a loud dissenter ordered back to Japan. Others were ordered back too such as Major-General Kotau Osuga, an artillery officer graduated from the Military Academy and the War College and former fortress commander of Chichi Jima. He, too, violently opposed Kuribayashi's changes and was relieved as commander of II Mixed Brigade.

A total of eighteen officers were sent home. After this, everyone began working together. Horie and Osuga relented somewhat; both feigned sickness in order to stay in Iwo Jima. Both died fighting.

Major-General Sadasue Senda took Osuga's command. Senda, a graduate from the Military Academy, formerly commanded the Sendai Reserve Military Academy and was well acquainted with infantry battle tactics. He not only fought the czar's troops early in the century in Manchuria. He later slaughtered thousands of Chinese at Nanking and Canton.

Lt. Col. Nishi, a baron, cavalry officer and old friend of Kuribayashi, arrived from North Manchuria with his XXVI Tank Regiment. They had only 13 tanks, having lost 28 when the USS Cobia sank the transport Nishu Maru. In spite of this setback, the tanks would be replaced later.

Rear-Admiral Toshinosuke Ichimaru, a Naval Academy graduate, limped badly from a 1926 plane crash and now commanded training units, mainly kamikazes. He wished to die in battle and now had his chance as head of the XXVII Air Wing. His numerous bombing raids against Saipan had been going well and here, closer to home, his fighters were scoring against the B-24s of the Seventh Air Force. Technically, he exercised overall control of the naval forces.

Captain Samajo Inouye commanded naval forces manning the anti-aircraft and coastal batteries. His anti-aircraft batteries had been doing well, too, in spite of damage by constant bombing. U.S. marines would have called him a real SOB; his men feared him. He was meaner than hell, a hard drinker and an excellent swordsman.

Colonel Masui Ikeda, commander of the 145th Infantry Div., was highly regarded by Kuribayashi. His faith was not misplaced. Ikeda's men held off the Marine Third Div. at airfield #2 for more than a week.

Captain Hoshio Yokoyama, an expert on the newly developed rocket guns, arrived in July with his crew and immediately placed 70 of the deadly weapons in areas designated by Kuribayashi.

All were top men, some older, some sent to Iwo, having outlived their usefulness in other areas, but all were experienced . . . and determined.

With 20,000 men working together, 135 pillboxes armed with 25mm machine guns were constructed around Chidori airfield in the first three months after the general's arrival. By the time of the invasion, 360 were complete and armed. Most of the island's 300 large anti-aircraft guns were depressed for regular artillery use. The smaller 75mm anti-aircraft guns served as anti-tank weapons.

Construction of the 18 miles of tunnels began immediately. Two of the airfields were operational, and work began on the third. An Army air squadron moved in, and units from Tateyama, Hachiiyo Jima and Chichi Jima arrived.

Supplying the island posed a major problem. There were two systems: Tokyo directly to Iwo by destroyer, high-speed transport or an SB, a vessel similar to the American *LST* but a bit smaller, or the other method, Tokyo to Chichi Jima, then to Haha Jima by sail or fishing boat, then a night dash to Iwo.

Darkness was imperative. More than 1500 men and 50,000 tons of material had been lost to submarines and planes. Landing supplies at Iwo's East Boat Basin was dangerous day or night, but perseverance prevailed.[4] By February 1, 1945, a 75-day food supply lay stored for the garrison of 22,000. With rationing, it could b extended to 120 days.

---

[4] Weapons included the following: 120 guns (larger than 75 mm), 100,000 rounds of ammunition; 300 anti-aircraft guns (75 mm), 500 rounds each; 20,000 small guns (up to 25 mm), including all machine guns, with 22 million rounds; 130 howitzers (8 and 12 cm), 90 rounds each; 20 mortars (20 cm), 50 rounds each; 70 rocket runs (20 cm), 50 rounds each; 40 anti-tank guns (47 mm), 600 rounds each; 20 anti-tank guns (37 mm), 500 rounds each; 27 tanks; at least 6 (.44 cal.) Smith & Wesson Model 3 revolvers.

Alligator Marines

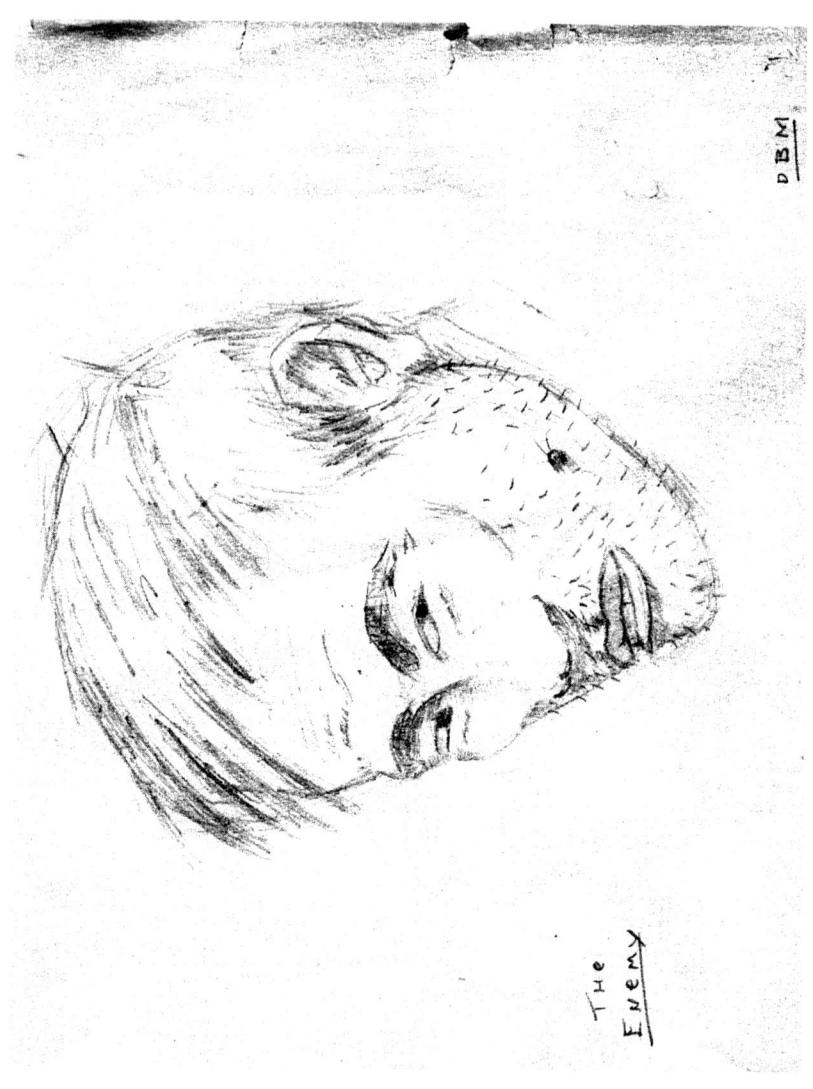

[*The enemy*]

Chapter 19: " . . I am proud and feel honored to fight until death comes . . ."[1]

Kuribayashi had no doubts he would be fighting Marines; he knew they were always given the toughest assignments. The General also predicted, quite correctly, that the landing would be made on the southeast Futatsune Beach, a strip of black sand 3600 yards wide at high tide, 4000 yards at low.

For him, there would be no victory. All on the island were doomed, but, if his men could inflict enough casualties, the Americans would be delayed and think twice before invading his homeland. Japan might also be able to negotiate a more honorable peace.

The units in the fortress ultimately consisted of the 9th through the 12th Independent Anti-tank battalions, and the 109th Division with the 20th Independent Mortar Battalion.

The 245th Infantry Regiment, 3rd Battalion, 17th Mixed Infantry Regiment, portions of the 2nd Mixed Brigade, the 204th Naval Constructions Btn., the 26th Tank Regiment, the 21st Special Machine Cannon Unit and the 2nd Mixed Brigade Field Hospital created a total of 22,000 men.

Baron Nishi's tanks were buried with only turrets exposed. They were to act as steel pillboxes and, after shooting as many attackers as possible, burst forth at the last possible minute to crush the enemy. The baron loudly decried the limited role his beloved tanks were to play.

Though the men were chronically short of everything, food, beer, saki, letters from home, and girls, and working under devastating conditions of constant air raids, shore bombardments and sickness, their morale, unbelievably, improved!

---

[1] Lt. Gen. Kurabayashi in a letter to his son Taro.

Airfields, continuously cratered by heavy bombs, were back in operation within hours. Fish, stunned by the heavy concussions, were eagerly snatched from the sea as a bonus to bland rations. Bomb-shattered wood was retrieved, reshaped and reused to construct more comfortable living quarters.

Underground facilities ranged form small chambers holding only a few men to cavernous garages, hospitals, hangars, mess halls and sleeping chambers. Ammunition, fuel, food and water were accessible by connecting tunnels. Passageways crossed and recrossed atop or below one another, some by three and four levels. One 540-yard tunnel near Chidori 1 ran 32 feet deep and had 17 entrances. Another, nearby, stretched 800 yards and had 14 entrances connected to huge blockhouses and pillboxes. The system allowed movement and communication from almost every point on the island. Mining engineers utilized natural ventilation by carving entrances at different levels, but still, some portions of the island were so hot and gassy that the men working underground had to wear gas masks. In these steaming areas work was limited to ten minutes a shift.

Many tunnels were electrified, some plastered. Entrances were angled at ninety degrees for protection against flamethrowers. In loose sand, tunnels consisted of empty gasoline drums with tops and bottoms removed. The drums were then welded end to end. They snaked in every direction, connecting the more remote blockhouses, bunkers and pillboxes. Most emplacements consisted of reinforced concrete walls and ceilings up to six feet thick. Each contained multiple openings and concealed passageways to allow covering fire in every direction and prevent entrapment.

Some dummy emplacements lay purposely set in exposed areas to entice attackers within firing range.

On the surface, rifle pits exposed muzzles only. Rocks, ravines and natural shadows were cleverly utilized to camouflage all firing positions. At no time, the general insisted, would his men be unnecessarily exposed.

". . I am proud and feel honored to fight until death comes . . ."1

Suribachi, the high point of the island, bristled with 115 large-caliber guns, all anchored in concrete. Two- and three-storied blockhouses and a thousand different caves on seven levels honeycombed this citadel of volcanic rock.

Under the watchful eye of Lt. Col. Nakane, a stickler on infantry discipline, rigid training combined with heavy labor kept the troops moving at a furious pace.

Over and over again, they practiced basic sniping from cave entrances, from behind rocks and hummocks; they crawled across open spaces and through ravines. They made mock attacks on their own positions, while the colonel or his umpires scored mistakes. The men raced through tunnels from pillbox to bunker, from entrance to entrance, each loaded with heavy ammunition or weapons. At stopping places, the panting, sweating men read and recited the list of "Courageous Battle Vows" pasted on the walls. More was expected of these men than of any other soldier in the world.

"We shall," the vows read, "dedicate ourselves and our entire strength to the defense of this island; we shall grasp bombs, charge enemy tanks and destroy them; we shall infiltrate into the midst of the enemy and annihilate them; with every salvo we will, without fail, kill the enemy; each man will make it his duty to kill ten of the enemy before dying; until we are destroyed to the last man we shall harass the enemy with guerrilla tactics."

This they vowed and this they did.

[*Japanese gun positions exposed and systematically destroyed.*]

Chapter 20: We have repulsed the enemy

American air raids against Iwo began August 10, 1944, in a half-hearted attempt to smash Iwo's airfields and prevent Jap bombers from slamming Saipan. The Japanese retaliated that month on the 12th, 15th and 19th with nine twin-engine Ki bombers; three were shot down.

Neither side seemed committed to a serious confrontation until America launched long-range B-29s against Tokyo. The superfort's airborne path to and from Japan crossed directly over Iwo's airspace, an open invitation that sent the island's pilots roaring from the runways. Though the fighters were unable to actively challenge the huge forts, they could, at least, pick off cripples and strays.

Why Iwo had to be captured

September and November brought more Japanese bombers to Saipan, the object being to blast the silver-bellied fortresses on the ground. Little damage was caused at first, but, on the 26th, an early morning raid scored by totaling one fort and severely damaging eleven others.

Flushed with success, the elated pilots raced home and made their report. Within minutes a second raid was launched. The daylight raid of November 27 garnered three more B-29s destroyed. Kuribayashi rejoiced at the added news that one of his planes had shot down one of the mammoth raiders returning from Tokyo and another bomber was forced to ditch in the sea.

December brought more raids and more losses to us, losses we could ill afford. Twenty-eight P-38s were dispatched from Saipan to strafe the sulfur island's ground targets. An hour later, 62 B-29s dropped 620 tons of bombs. At noon, 102 B-24s followed with 194 more tons. The Navy sent three heavy cruisers and six destroyers to pound 2500 rounds of eight-inch high explosives and 5334 rounds of five-inch shells into the island fortress.

The general's gun silently endured the relentless bombardment. The attackers sailed off, smugly satisfied that they had effectively and forever destroyed the enemy.

Kuribayashi's cunning strategy and effective defenses paid off. Not a single casualty resulted from the heavy shelling. Within 24 hours, both airstrips were fully operational. Reconnaissance photos revealed that Iwo's defenses grew more formidable with each passing day. Yet, strangely enough, the large number of troops known to be on the island seemed to be diminishing. It was maddening.

[*Heavy shelling had little effect*]

Two more Navy shellings by cruisers in December delivered 1500 eight-inch explosive rounds. They smashed two small ships anchored in the East Boat Basin and again pockmarked both airfields. The following day, Japanese fighters and bombers roared off Iwo's repaired strips and headed straight for Saipan. They bagged four B-29s and damaged eleven more.

Obviously, Iwo must be captured. The huge battle wagon *Indiana* steamed up and pounded the island with 203 rounds of legendary, 2,700-pound, sixteen-inch shells. Two more ships were sunk. Then, cruisers moved in to slam another 1,300 eight-inch shells into the quaking island. This assault was followed by low-flying B-24s dropping another 700 tons of bombs, while cruisers fired 23,000 rounds of five-inch ordnance to ice the rocky cake. The Japanese simply dug deeper and waited.

For ten weeks, Iwo was bombed on a daily basis

Allied transports in Hawaii, the States, Guam and Saipan began taking on machines, weapons, fuel, food, medicines and thousands of men for the coming battle. Few of these actions remained secret, and Kuribayashi was aware, almost to the day, when to expect attack. For ten weeks, Iwo was bombed on a daily basis; yet the stubborn Japs continued raiding Saipan up until January 5, 1945. On the 16th of February six battleships, four heavy cruisers, one light cruiser and sixteen destroyers surrounded the Japanese stronghold for a final pre-invasion softening up. The command ship divided the island's less-than-eight-square-mile surface into 700 numbered squares, each square a target of a specific ship. After a prescribed time of firing, each ship was to signal its target destroyed and the corresponding square would be crossed off the plotting board.

Battlewagons, veterans of North Africa and Normandy campaigns, *Nevada, Texas, Arkansas,* and *New York,* plus *Idaho* and *Tennessee,* accompanied by heavy cruisers *Pensacola, Tuscaloosa, Salt Lake City* and *Chester,* plus the light cruiser *Vicksburg,* opened up with a vengeance on command. Two hundred and three sixteen-inch shells roared into Iwo's defenses at 2,000 miles per hour. The smaller ships followed with 6,472 eight-inch and 15,221 five-inch shells.

A Zero rose from the island, attacked a slow spotter plane, overshot and was downed as it passed in front of the surprised pilot's guns. It was the only real victory on this hot, sweaty day, for, when the smoke cleared, exhausted naval crews were stunned to find only seventeen of their 700 targets crossed off.

Iwo Jima appeared dead

The following morning, minesweepers, under the protection of the heavy cruiser *Pensacola*, swept the area. They found no mines and, except for a few random 40mm shots, and the taking of one hit by the *Tennessee* that wounded four men, they encountered no heavy enemy fire. The *Pensacola* moved in close. Still no fire. Observers on the bridge detected no movement on the island. Iwo Jima appeared dead. The cruiser sniffed, hound dog style, to within 1600 yards of the black beach. Suddenly, all hell broke loose. In three minutes *Pensacola's* observation plane was blasted from its catapult, the ship's information center lay in shambles and ready ammo exploded below deck when, one after the other, six 150mm shells fired from a hidden emplacement below Suribachi slammed into her. The executive officer and sixteen men died; 120 were wounded. The firing ceased as suddenly as it began. The crack Japanese artillerymen would have done more damage had not the concrete base of their heavy weapon given way. Their gun captain wept.

Admiral Ichimaru, made a fatal mistake

At 1030 hours, 13 *LCIs* slowly approached the eastern shore to assist Navy frogmen chart and destroy underwater obstructions and plant fathom markers. Assuming the approaching gunships were carrying the actual landing forces, Kuribayashi's naval officer, Admiral Ichimaru, made a fatal mistake in this masterful waiting game.

He ordered his hidden guns to fire. Light and heavy guns answered with alacrity and amazing accuracy. Within seconds, every ship in the advance line sustained one or more hits.

Fourteen six-inch shells slammed into *LCI 474,* setting off three magazine explosions and four fires. Forty-three seamen were killed and 153 wounded. She went to the bottom with six engineers trapped in the engine room.

Japanese radio operators listened and gleefully reported the plain language traffic:

"473 on fire sinking rapidly."

"450 40mm gun mounts down, we're on fire."

"457 . . . sinking."

"466 needs tow."

"Tennessee, Nevada, Idaho, lay smoke over that damned beach. Destroyers, increase your fire. Get an air strike on the base of that mountain. Nevada, move in and pound that mountain."

Sharpshooting Japanese killed 21 and wounded 18 aboard *LCI 449* by picking men off her gun platforms, conning tower and bridge.

LCI 473 burst into flame after taking 189 hits in her hull.

LCI 450 suffered hits in her hull and gun mounts. Her anchor chain was severed, and the anchor plunged to the bottom. This gave birth to the grim joke that she was the first ship to drop anchor in Japanese home waters.

Even the destroyer *Leutze* took a hit that killed seven and wounded thirty-three. In short, twelve U.S. ships were hit; nine were put out of commission and one sunk.

In spite of the carnage, the mission was carried out, and the little vessels continued to recover the frogmen. Of one hundred swimmers in the water, only one went missing, however several were severely wounded while being picked up.[1]

The Japanese believed they had repulsed an invasion and smugly reported the news to Tokyo. Commander in Chief of the

---

[1] The next day, while relaxing aboard their ship APD <u>Blessman</u>, eighteen of the frogmen were killed and twenty-seven wounded by two Jap aerial bombs. <u>Blessman</u>'s crew suffered a like amount.

Combined Imperial Fleet, Admiral Soemu Toyoda, congratulated Ichimaru: "Despite very powerful enemy bombings and shellings, your unit at Iwo Jima cooly judged the enemy intentions and foiled the first landing attempt and serenely awaits the next one, determined to hold Iwo at any cost. I am greatly elated to know that, and I wish you to continue to maintain high morale and repulse the enemy, no matter how intense the attacks, and safeguard the outer defenses of our homeland."

In the firm belief that this was the first time Marines had ever been pushed off an island, Radio Tokyo crowed, "On February 17, in the morning, enemy troops tried to land on the island of Iwo. The Japanese garrison at once attacked these troops and repelled them into the sea. Five enemy warships, including a battleship, were sunk."

Kuribayashi, peering down from his observation post atop hill 382, smiled grimly. In spite of this minor success and the congratulatory message, he was not happy that several of his well-concealed gun positions had been exposed and were now being systematically destroyed.

It was pretty plain to both sides that Japanese firepower, with the exception of the artillerymen who gave away their hidden positions, was scarcely fazed.

Chapter 21: The Marines are coming...

On Sunday, with the scheduled landing only 24 hours away, the frustrated attackers revised their strategy. Forty-two Saipan-based B-24s raked the island with bombs and dropped over 100 fifty-gallon drums of napalm. They accomplished little.

New York and *Nevada* now directed their fire to the beach, while *Tennessee* avenged her Pearl Harbor wounds by carving up the cliff emplacements on Hill 382. *Idaho* moved south to pound Suribachi. Every suspicious mound was stripped of its cover; if concrete showed, it was pulverized.

Previous shelling forced Kuribayashi to rebase his bombers to the north on Chichi Jima, but he still had Zero fighter planes in hidden revetments on Chidori #2. They were wheeled out, armed with bombs, and the pilots instructed to ram the battlewagons. One of the pilots demurred, claiming he had a headache; another took his place. Both planes barely lifted off before meeting a hailstorm of fire. The Zeros splashed into the sea without doing any harm.

The day's tally for the attackers amounted to only three destroyed blockhouses out of twenty and only six or so of the dozens of pillboxes.

Admiral Blandy radioed Admiral Turner, "I believe landing can be accomplished tomorrow."

Lt. Col. Don Weller requested another day for bombardment

There were still hundreds of guns left untouched, and every battleship had tons of ammunition waiting to be fired. It was a tough decision: Clear the beach defenses and the coast guns commanding the beach now. Marine gunfire officer Lt. Col. Don Weller requested another day at least for bombardment.

"Never mind the artillery," Weller bitterly wrote, *"Never mind the mortars and anti-aircraft guns undestroyed, never mind the inland blockhouses and pillboxes that would bar the way later."* The Marine officer's request was denied.

There would be *no* extra day.

Firing began at dawn on the 19th, with two battleships on the west coast and five on the east. Each was allotted 75 rounds followed by cruisers launching 100 rounds. Time was called to allow 120 rocket-firing planes to swoop the island. At 0805 the battleships again pounded the island, this time with 155 rounds apiece; cruisers again moved in and fired 150 rounds of eight-inch ordnance, followed by destroyers with 500 rounds of five-inch shells. All ships ceased fire at 0850 to allow another seven-minute aircraft strafing run. Two minutes later, *LST* rocket ships launched a deadly fury of 20,000 screaming rockets each. The island, obscured by smoke and dust, remained silent.

One minute later 68 lumbering *LVTs*, some armed with 75mm cannon, charged through the surf to disgorge 1,360 fighting leathernecks onto the black, shifting, lava sands of Iwo Jima's eastern beach.

The first wave of Marines met only scattered small-arms fire, mostly machine gun and mortar. The lightly armored, slow-moving Alligators became easy targets as they bogged down in the soft volcanic ash. A few of the tractors managed to crest the ten to fifteen-foot sloping terraces, but none made it beyond fifty yards inland.

The first three waves of Alligators were followed by wave after wave of varied landing craft that sped or crawled shoreward to be greeted with minimal fire, just enough to make the men wary. Within forty-five minutes, the beach overflowed in a massive traffic jam. Boats, tractors, jeeps, men, and tons of war material jammed the beach.

Kuribayashi watched with great satisfaction as the surf became more turbulent, causing numerous *LCVPs* to swamp.

Each waterlogged hulk hampered the approach of succeeding waves of boats and tractors, which in turn swamped or bogged and blocked the big *LSTs* carrying heavy tanks and large-caliber guns. Soon, with the exception of a few regimental combat teams inching their way forward, 9000 men thronged a beachhead less than fifty yards deep.

This was the moment the Japanese had sweat for

It was the moment Lt. Gen. Tadamichi Kuribayashi had been awaiting. In spite of earlier opposition from every quarter, his efforts would now pay off. On his command, multi-colored flares arced over the packed humanity on the beach below. This was the moment his officers and men had worked and sweat for, the signal for every weapon to open fire.

They promptly obeyed the order.

Japanese gunners had already targeted every inch of the beach. Enfilading fire from the north, Hill 382, pounded the 4th Marine Division crammed on Yellow 1 and 2, Blue 1 and 2 eastern beach sectors. The artillerymen on Suribachi then raked back and forth through the 27th and 28th Battalions of the 5th Division landing on Green, Red and portions of Yellow beaches. Fire from Hill 382 did the same, while frontal fire from the neck of the island fanned from one end of the beach to the other. Suribachi was a frowning fort, essentially a fifty-story building with cannons poking out of every window.

To the north end of the landing beach sat Hill 382 and Motoyama, thirty stories high, bristling with cannon. Because of the crowded beach, inexperienced cannoneers found aiming unnecessary. Just load and fire as quickly as possible. The veteran artillerymen, nevertheless, took their time; they were very accurate.

[*My troops. First Wave.
View from cab of my tractor.*[

Chapter 22: "Four days? This will be like shooting ducks."

Oh, yeah? Well, these ducks will be shooting back." (overheard aboard *LST 789*)

It was D-day minus one, the weather pleasant. The last few days aboard *LST 789* from Saipan had been uneventful. Lt. Charles Schultz ordered me to paint over the Jap flags I had painted on my helmet. The Marine emblem on the front of my helmet was O.K. but the painted flags were not. They were my score card; if pilots could keep a record of their kills, I thought I could, too. Schultz didn't agree. I suppose he was still upset about the colored tractors.

Our crewmen Joe Casillas and Ted Klein constantly inspected binding chains holding the tractor in place on the metal deck of the ship. Frank Rhoads checked his radio equipment on a daily basis, while I hand cranked the engine 42 revolutions to ensure against piston lock when using the starter. It was up to me to continually check oil and fuel and make certain there were no leaks or other problems. A stalled vehicle on that crowded deck would be chaos on D-day. Sgt. Walt "Stoney" Gragg, crew chief, entered all results in the log. Every day, when the ship's ventilators were actuated, one-half of the tractors in the belly of the *LST* would test run their engines. The noise of those big 250-hp Continentals was ear splitting.

We had been briefed on landing sites, told we would be there four days and make two trips, one to bring in troops and one to bring in supplies. We would then re-embark and move on to the big island, Okinawa. That's where the real fighting was going to be.We had steak for breakfast

We had steak for breakfast.

Not everyone ate, but those who did, it was steak for breakfast. Some of the boys attended church services and others worried about stomach wounds, but I couldn't pass up a meal like that; the cooks did a great job.

We went below early. Stoney and I lay atop the cab of our tractor, number 66, and played chess until the alarm sounded. He folded the miniature board; we'd finish the game later. I stripped off my khaki shirt and kept only my dungaree jacket. My tanker jacket, I thought, as I had sewn on extra pockets to hold candy bars and stuff. The men of the 25th Regt. 4th Div. clambered into the tractors. The massive *LST* doors ground open, fresh air gushed in, we got the flashing "GO" light and Stoney signaled to engage and move out.

The screeching of metal on metal, as hundreds of growsers on seventeen pairs of tank tracks ground into the steel deck, ceased only when the last tractor scraped down the ramp into the sea. The cab sweltered even though the sun just rose but it was clear sailing for rendezvous and wave formation. The tractor ran perfectly. Frank sat next to me, relaying orders from Stoney above. As close as we were, it was impossible to hear anything without earphones because of the engine noise directly behind us and the huge transmission grinding between us.

Only the sight of the smoking island in front of us could be seen through the small slit in the armor. Suddenly we plunged amid a lot of floating wreckage; we hadn't known about the ships being battered the day before. Frank thought we had entered a floating mine field. As he squinched his eyes against the anticipated explosion, a chuckle escaped my lips. I snuffed a cigarette needing both hands for the controls as we ground in close. A nagging feeling warned me something was wrong, something I couldn't put my finger on.

Stoney cautioned me to slow down as we propelled ahead of the pack. The radio crackled . . .

"AA and AB from AJ (C.O. Shead), keep line dressed up, you are ahead, go to right when you hit beach."

0815.

"Four days? This will be like shooting ducks." "

"AJ to AC [" C " Company] *You will have to go around tin cans and battle wagons.*

"Keep lined up; you are bunched up."

"AJ to AB ["B" Company], *you are too far left."*

Unknown: *"Baker company is never on station anyway . . . they are always off."*

Unknown: *"Baker 6, 7 and 8, guide to right."*

"C" Company may have been a bit too far left. Second Armored was supposed to be in front of us; I spotted a couple of their tanks off to the right but none in front of us. Stoney radioed me again "*Slow down.*"

Suddenly, the surf sloshed against our sides. Maneuvering through the waves we felt the growsers dig in. It was probably the best landing I ever made. Not wanting the men to drop off the ramp into deep water and drown, I hollered at Stoney, "Don't drop the ramp!" Gunning the engine, we crawled up slowly, still not sure how far to go. The tracks didn't seem right. I waffled the tracks and double clutched; then we made it over the second terrace. We pitched about 75 feet from the surf. The men could safely disembark.

My watch said 8:57.

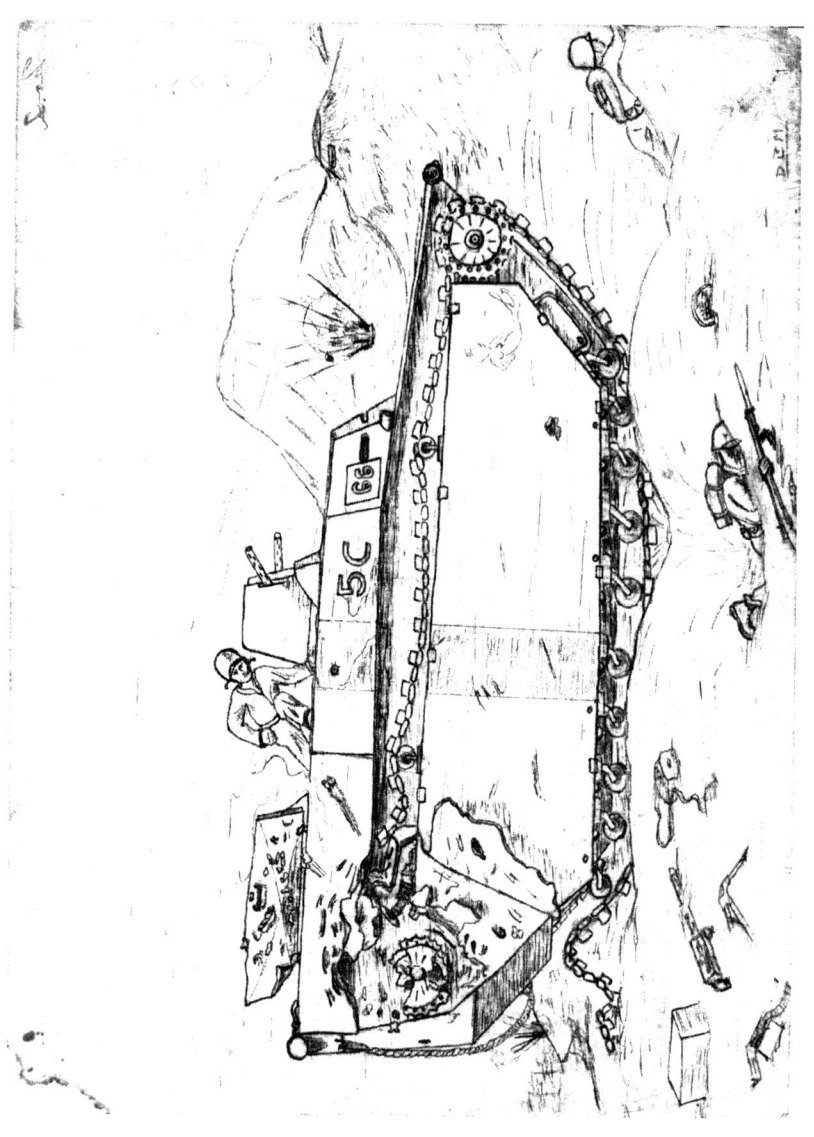

[*Last one out, me! Blue Beach*]

"Four days? This will be like shooting ducks."

Chapter 23: Impossible to remember but impossible to forget

Alphabet designations and code names were used in 5th Amph. radio transmissions to confuse the enemy, but they seemingly didn't confuse anyone except us.

"A" stood for Astonish, the 5th Amphs. AJ was our battalion headquarters or C.O. Major Shead. The major was also called Shadrack; Captain Stoll was, of course, "Baldy;" Lt. Sumner, "Bigfoot;" Lt. Wilson, "Tattoo;" Lt. Bill Clark, "Skinny;" Art Haas, "Pooper;" Lt. Carl Lauer, "Tex;" Lt. Mark Retter, "Marker." AA would be "A" Company C.O., and AB designated "B" company, and so forth.

"AA to AJ, on the beach 9:04 no casualties yet . . .

"AB to AJ, on beach!"

"AC to AJ, on beach! "

My watch stopped; it still showed 8:57. Machine gun fire raked the upper portion of our tractor, number 66 named Margie June after a girl friend of one of the crew. Bullets slammed Margie June's armor hard. I watched through the slit as her headlights disappeared in a shower of glass and metal.

"AJ to all units, track numbers 7 and 24 hit."

Unknown: *"Negative, 24 OK . . . but 26 is hit . . . 7 is Bigfoot."*

This confused my buddies, as they called me Bigfoot because of my shoe problem on Saipan. However, in this case Big Foot was Lt. Paul Sumner in tractor number 7.

"A to AJ, any news of B 67?"

"Negative. "

"All units, AJ needs casualty and tractor reports as soon as possible."

127

Alligator Marines

The small arms fire from the airfield directly in front increased, as did the mortars. This volley didn't concern me as much as my determination to allow the troops to disembark on dry land. I didn't move the tractor until a troop run directly in front of my cab and blasted a rifle grenade into a very low concrete bunker. Thirty combat-ready men of the 23rd Regiment, 4th Division, swarmed alongside and then past us, attempting to top the terrace. With the vehicle emptied, I felt better.

Joe and Ted raised the ramp while Stoney manned the machine gun. We were empty. We actually would have had the dog through this, because originally, Marcus Gutierrez had been assigned to our tractor. But he had a last-minute change to Kennedy's tractor so Samson, our dog, went with them. Stoney gave the "all clear" to move out.

Heavy machine gun fire, and possibly some 20mm stuff, reigned down on us now. I engaged reverse gear. The engine roared. *Nothing* happened. I tried first gear then double clutched but again with no success.

"Stoney, I hollered, "are the troops clear? Maybe we can spin in place." He shouted they were. Even ramming the shift lever in every gear; nothing worked. The transmission bands overheated. We would have to shut down for a cooling-off period, not a good situation because other waves pounded in behind us.

"A to A3, Baker 6 landed in mortar fire . . . B 4 is OK."

"A to AJ, 49 is on beach on my left flank and is out of action . . . crew safe. A 7 seems to be sunk, crew status undetermined."

"AD to AJ 14 is floating around . . . 49 knocked out . . . 51 is missing."

"Al to AJ looking for 35, 56, 58, 66, 86, and 5 ... have casualties, need help!"

"AK to AJ, 7 LVTs on beach . . . no, there are 7 blown up!"

"Four days? This will be like shooting ducks." "

"AMI to AJ, believe three men dead, one on *hospital ship."*

"Marshall, Rhoads . . . !" Stoney yelled while pounding a wrench on the armor. "Get out of there. ABANDON. ABANDON!"

I sure as hell wasn't going to be killed by my own radioman

A 47mm demolished the rear sprocket of our tractor rendering the overheated transmission a pointless concern. Frank fired his .45 automatic at the radio. The huge slug ricocheted off the metal face bouncing around the cab.

"Knock it off, " I yelled, "your shooting is worse than the Jap fire outside." He answered he had to destroy the radio in case of capture. "Fuck the radio!" With that, I barreled out the small escape hatch into the cargo compartment. *I* sure as hell wasn't going to be killed by my own radioman. Rhoads had to climb over the hot transmission, but he made it out, too without any more inside shooting.

Inside the cargo compartment Ted and Joe unwrapped rations and grenades. The ramp had been cranked up and was now stuck because of shell damage. Stoney explained that when the shell hit, the blast blew into the tool compartment and flung wrenches around like shrapnel.

Concussions from the thunderous racket outside bounced our tractor back and forth. Half our radio antenna disappeared while the unshot portion twanged back and forth. Sand bags, meant to be thrown atop lobbed grenades, lined the inside of the cargo area. Suddenly the tractor rocked with a loud crack. I pulled my shirt off and felt sand running down my bare back. A 47mm armor-piercing shell had penetrated our half-inch armor just above my head. It passed through the sand bags, knocked the pistol grip off our .30 turret machine gun and continued through the armor on the other side without exploding.[1] Had it

---

[1]

not been for that thin armor, the round would have exploded in the cargo area and killed us all.

Wiggling back into the smoky cab, I grabbed my dungaree jacket. Because the ramp could not be lowered, we were fully exposed while scrambling up and over the side. We took turns, Frank leapt over on one side; one minute later Ted leapt off the other. Joe, then Stoney; I went last. The minute I hit ground it was obvious what had caused the track problem; we had bogged in the soft black sand. Unlike regular beach sand, this stuff offered no resistance. You could push your doubled-up fist into it clear to the elbow. Everything and everybody sank into the damn stuff.

Running toward a blasted pillbox on the right proved difficult. It was like wallowing in knee-deep mud or dry quicksand. Half running and half crawling I struggled some 10 yards to the concrete blockhouse and barreled in through the twisted reinforcing rods. Stoney and four other Marines pulled me into the crowed room. Three dead Japanese sardined us together. I sat on one of the Japs and caught my breath. A shell hit the thick concrete roof. A fine powder filtered down. Stoney clutched a small pocket Bible. This surprised me as he, like me, didn't believe in anything. The Bible lay open, but I don't think he read it. I nudged his knee and mentioned that the book was upside down.

Someone told me it snowed just four days prior. I regretted leaving my khaki shirt aboard the *LST*. Now, with Margie June out of action, I would not likely get back to the ship for a few

---

The rounds that got our tank were fired from the base of the cliff of Hill 382. In one of General Kuribayashi's dispatches to Tokyo, he cited a Lieutenant Nakamura for operating his anti-tank weapon alone, after his entire crew were killed by naval gunfire. The general further stated the brave man had knocked out two score tanks in three days. Later, I examined his gun position. Judging from the angle of the hits on #66, I have no doubt it was this man who so accurately picked us off. He died at his post on the third day.

days. I noticed the guy upon whom I sat was rather large for a Japanese, about my size. He wore a fairly clean, white silk shirt; alongside him lay a regular blue, woolen Jap Navy jumper. The jumper would have been warmer, but I didn't want to be mistaken for a member of the Japanese Navy. I seized the silk shirt.

What the hell, I thought, why not? Even though a bit tight when the weather got bad later, I felt lucky to have it.

Our shelter took two more direct hits. The crack Japanese artillerymen had zeroed in on their own positions. I didn't like being cooped up doing nothing.

Radio messages over command net:

1036 (From 25 Marines) Catching hell from the quarry. Heavy mortar and machine gun fire.

1039 (From 23rd Marines) taking heavy casualties and can't move for the moment. Mortars killing us.

1042 (From 27th Marines) All units pinned down by artillery and mortars. Casualties heavy. Need tank support fast to move anywhere.

1046 (From 28th Marines) Taking heavy fire and forward movement stopped. Machine gun and artillery fire heaviest ever seen.

"I'm going out," I told Stoney. He advised me to wait until things calmed and that maybe we could catch a tractor back to the *LST*.

With an overblown dose of bravado I replied, "They couldn't be getting more fire than we're getting here and I can kill some Japs."

This island didn't have a goddamned tree, blade of grass or even a coconut to hide behind

Crawling out into a small revetment leading away from the beach, that nagging feeling returned. At the top of the ditch at the third level, was the answer. All my self-imposed jungle training, the hours of concealment, the camouflage, the miles of crawling through dense underbrush at Pendleton and Saipan trying to be the best jungle fighter in the Corps, wasn't worth a dime. This island didn't have a god damned tree, blade of grass or even a coconut to hide behind. No wonder High Command didn't care about my blue tractors. What a stupid island.

Sand belching alongside my head, jolted me back to reality. A Jap machine gunner zeroed in with a short burst. I backed down . . . *fast*. A lieutenant, leading his squad, crawled up behind me. He wouldn't listen to my warning about the gunner. The lieutenant and two of his men tumbled back, dead.

The bombardment increased leaving the beach in complete chaos and wreckage littering every square foot. Movement of vehicles or boats wasn't possible. I pushed back into the pillbox and scratched a hole for myself, but, when a chunk of thigh plopped in, I tossed it back out. Then I moved out, too.

The first enemy barrage wiped out the entire Shore Fire Control Party of the 3rd Battalion, 25th Marines.

Amid horrendous noise, impossible to describe, I returned to my original plan to move forward. Crawling past the bunker directly in front of Margie June, I found a Browning automatic rifle (BAR) beside a dead Marine. While taking his bandoleers, the infantry knocked out the gunner who had nearly nailed me earlier. I joined up with them. We crossed the moonscape under intense fire at half jog, half ground hog.

It seemed hours before we reached the north end of the first airfield. Fire power barraged us; enemy pillboxes supported each other from every direction. It was either the 25th or maybe the 23rd that I had joined. Trying to cross a ditch called a long tank trap, the captain directed us to fire into every visible port as fast as possible. This way a squad of our men could advance. On signal, they ducked; the rest of us lobbed grenades. Under the smoke, a man sprang up and shoved in a satchel charge through the nearest gun port. A huge explosion finished that bunker but there were a thousand more just like it.

It was rough distinguishing night from day

The sequence of events, even remembering night from day, is hazy. Nights shown bright as day due to thousands of flares flung skyward by both sides. Never-ending noise, dust, muddy rain, get up, run, flop down, fire, shoot that son-of-a-bitch, heads up, incoming fire, constant fatigue . . .no, you felt too damned tired to be fatigued.

"Duke, can you operate a flame thrower?" The question jolted me; I'd forgotten my nickname was printed on my jacket. A hand clasped my shoulder. I shook my head no.

"Your jacket, you're not one of our guys." The lieutenant almost cried. "For Christ's sake tell me you can! Our man is dead. I'll detail someone to carry it for you."

It was the one weapon I had no training in.

"I'm an Alligator man." my voice uttered regretfully. "But, I sure as hell know where some bazooka ammo is, about twelve rounds. On the deck of my tractor. The guys forgot it when they left."

"Get it," he barked and pointed to another, "you help." I handed over my BAR, and the two of us turned toward the beach. It took about forty-five minutes. *The ramp still would not lower*. Rotten luck. Consequently, I tossed rounds over the side. These rounds weighed about six pounds apiece and were a bastard to carry. My companion garnered an armload and took off. I ducked into the cab. Rhoads' pistol shot had only damaged one dial on the radio, and the set still worked despite the shot off antenna.

[*Minefields*]

Chapter 24: This is as bad as it can get, but don't bet on it

D day, 12:30 hours.

"A to AJ, 55 has second gear and clutch gone . 56 and 58 are OK."

"AL to AJ, number 49 and 51 on beach . crew 51 missing."

"AJ to AK, 2nd armored needs ammo."

"AK to AJ, we have no 75 ammo, have 6 boxes of .30 caliber . . . 4 boxes of .30 cal ball . . . 6 boxes 66mm mortar . . . 10 boxes frag grenades . . . 8 boxes 80mm mortar . . . 2 boxes carbine . . . we will send it all."

"AJ to AM1, any news of 7 and Big Foot?"

"AM1 to AJ, believe Big Foot dead, and most of crew."[1]

"AJ to AK, number 92 appears to be on way to beach . . . should not be there . . . send him back."

"AA to AJ, need bazooka ammo immediately."

Things did not look good for the tractor men, or anyone else for that matter. Art Steinbruner blew clear out of his tractor. The explosion peeled his boots right off his feet. Knocked silly, Art never-the-less survived.

I had some Lifesavers, of all things

Earlier I'd stashed some candy in the cab, *Lifesavers* of all things. How ironic! Stuffing the Lifesavers into my breast pocket, I grappled with the remainder of bazooka ammo and twisted my way through the blasted wreckage to catch up to my ammo-carrying buddy. The rough surf besplashed everything. Big ships falteringly thrust through the wreckage to unload. The

---

[1] Unfortunately, this was true. Lt. Sumner and his crew, with the exception of Frank Hadley, were killed by a direct mortar hit.

day turned cold and sopping wet. Even though sweating, my new silk shirt became a plus.

A newly arrived squad headed in the same direction as me when an onslaught caught us. We scattered. A stone-lined rifle pit big enough for one man promised shelter. Hesitation saved me. Another Marine dove in. Maybe the pit was mined or received a direct hit by mortar, but the explosion threw half his body, with helmeted head, right arm, neck and a portion of his chest, into the air. It landed a few feet away, the open eyes stared directly at me, the rest of him gone.

Lesson learned. From then on, newly exploded holes became my preference. A still smoking hole is obviously safe from booby traps. Sliding into a crater; another man jumped in after me. His pale and stricken face appeared about to retch. He peered down at four severed fingers in the bottom of the crater while pressing against the side of the hole. "Get over here, I told him, "the fire is coming from my side." He appeared confused for a moment, then recognized the value of my statement. He thought me a real gung-ho veteran and crawled over fingers and all to crouch and smoke with me. Ah, nothing seems as satisfying as a cigarette when under shellfire.

Eventually, the bazooka rounds were delivered. A sergeant (the captain and lieutenant both dead by then) asked if I could get more and some water, too. They needed water *bad*.

Fighting is thirsty work and getting wounded causes a greater thirst. Both reasons applied to these guys. Five gallons remained in the tractor so I turned back toward the beach. Strange, I wanted to prove myself a fighting Marine; instead, I became a water boy, a gofer. But, orders are orders. Again, I headed for Margie June..

Along the way a wounded Marine called out, "Can you give me a hand?" A bubble of intestine protruded from his abdomen. In the movies wounded are always screaming in agony hyping up the audience. I did not find this with our wounded. If able to talk they were usually cursing up a storm, something like "God dammit, *look what them bastards did, of all the god damn luck.*" More than once I marveled at this attitude.

He wasn't quite sure what to do. "With a wound like that, I dare not shoulder-carry you." He nodded in agreement. I opened the little aid pouch, laid a 4 x 4 pad over the wound, soaked it with water and left him my canteen. He'd soon need all the water he could get if I couldn't get help back to him.

[*Water to wounded and me running to get more*]

Burning tractors littered the beach and it occurred to me that my troops were mostly down. The *LCMs* tried desperately to unload heavy tanks; some already bogged in the soft black sand. The barrage along the shore appeared worse, if that was possible. Our 2nd armored caught hell. Their tractors were the old *LVT-2s* with a 75mm cannon and turret planted on top. Only the turret could be considered armored and even that was open on top. The *LVT-2-A's* were excellent mobile gun platforms but they also made great targets.

Time 1330

Alligator Marines

"AJ to AA92. Tell Phosgene to report to Blue 2 control instead of going in."

"AM to AJ. Cupie has 15 serviceable LVTs on beach . . . one dead, two wounded."

"AL to AJ. Number 61 is on beach . . . 60 not around us . . . 49 now missing."

"AJ to AK. Number 92 is on the loose. ... ordered to *Blue 2* . . . headed toward LSM."

"A92 to AJ. Am unloading ammo *on beach.*"

"AJ to Jo Jo. Locate LSR 764 . . . . taJcke *10 LVTs and load with ammo and report to me on the beach.*"

Small waves of *LCVPs* poked their noses against the beach. Work parties snaked heavy lines to their sterns in an attempt to prevent broaching and capsizing in the pounding surf. But, as soon as the lines pulled taut, shells cascaded in, killing or wounding more of the work party. The boats, their crews and needed supplies foundered into the raging surf.

Inching toward the beach, the exposed nose of an aerial bomb poked through the black sand which had blown away. I glanced around. Another. And another! The whole place was a minefield. My weight couldn't set these off, I hoped, but tanks or trucks, obviously, couldn't get through.

Momentarily, my original mission took a back seat. Picking up a rifle, I jammed it upright in the ground as a warning post, then ran from hole to hole, picked up Garands and carbines and stuck them wherever I saw a mine.

Sappers, their faces covered with white cream, were crawling up from the beach probing with bayonets locating and deactivating mines. Iwo's black sands contained enough metallic qualities to make metal detectors useless. I waved and caught their attention. I pointed to the marked bombs. The men acknowledged with a return wave.

Another problem plagued me. For a driver, leggings weren't necessary, and I hadn't been issued any. Without protection, gritty ash crammed into my shoes at every step. Finally, the pain stopped me. I sat and emptied my new boots; it felt great to take them off. Could I go barefoot again? Better sense prevailed. I removed leggings from a fallen Marine, laced them on my legs and continued on.

Miss Tokyo Rose, Moby Dick, Little Orphan Annie

Once in the cab of Margie June, I turned on the radio. This time I got, of all things, popular music broadcast from Tokyo via the Jap station here on Iwo.

"Hello, all you poor Marines trying to land on Iwo. This is Little Orphan Annie. Do you know that a 4F in your town is now out with the girl you left behind?"

. Little Orphan Annie then played Glenn Miller's "Moonlight Serenade." The music offered a moment of replete before spinning the dial to pick up our people again.

"AJ to all units, I can't tell what is going on at Blue beach 2...too much smoke...what is going on...need info...come in on air...all units, I need to know what is going on.... " *"Unknown. "If you want to know what is going on get your ass in here and find out ..."*

"AJ identify..I'll hang the man who said that!"

Silence

"AF to AA. Number 95 [Little] and 20 [Brock and Wester] abandoned on Blue 2 . . J think crews are safe ... am *checking."*

"AJ to all units. Where is LST 711? . . . Hartwell, Brace and Metcalf are reported missing."

Shells exploded overhead; shrapnel rained down on the tractor creating a racket. Someone earlier mentioned that rain detonated the shells, but someone else countered by saying they were timed to explode in the air to get a wider killing pattern on the ground. Not sure, I figured it was too hot here. Grabbing the water can, I started out but then an idea struck me and I returned to the radio. A male voice now spoke on the Jap station; he called himself Moby Dick, a turncoat, I suppose. Well, I'd put him to good use.

"Wouldn't *you Marines,*" he blabbered, *"like to be home now enjoying fresh bread with real margareene?"* (I cracked up because the dumbbell couldn't even pronounce margarine.) *"Well, you won't be able to enjoy anything, because you will all be dead soon. Yes, men of the 4th and 5th Division, and let's not forget the 23rd Combat teams and 5th Amphibious Tractors, and all you others who are going to die soon. Look what your leaders have gotten you into. But, in the mean time, try to enjoy the music. Don't forget this is Moby Dick and* I *told you so.* "

All right, you son-of-a-bitch, we'll enjoy it. I opened the hatches, turned up the volume as loud as possible and, until the battery ran down, the men on the beach heard music by Benny Goodman, Glenn Miller and other popular bands, compliments of Miss Tokyo Rose, Moby Dick, Little Orphan Annie and all the rest of their little helpers.

Not to stay in the open too long, I dove in a hole and joined another Marine. Unlike me, he wore full combat gear, pack and everything. Machine gun fire immediately pinned us down. While crouched he growled, "as soon as this gunner stops we'll get mortar fire." I figured as a seasoned campaigner, he must know more than me. "When the gun stops, I'll count to three, you go out that way; I'll go out here." I agreed. the firing stopped, he counted, "*One, Two, Three.*" KAPOOM came a terrific explosion. I floundered backward in the hole. My companion knelt in an upright position as if ready to spring out. Frozen in place, clutching his rifle, his head, helmet and everything above his lower jaw vanished! The first mortar round had hit right in front of him. Returning the next day, I threw a poncho over the body. I didn't even know his name.

Chapter 25: The careful application of terror is also a form of communication

"AJ *to all units. LST 731 too far to left . .. right . . . tell skipper on LST to move now, dammit!"*

"*AA to AJ. We are fifty percent unloaded.*"

"*B6 to AJ. Several tractors near me are burning . . am returning and will check on fuel.*"

"*AJ to all units. Need small ammo on beach!*"

"*AL to AJ. Crew of 31 safe.*"

"*AJ to AC. Send Olkieweicz to LST 787... needed immediately.* "

"*B6 to* AF. *Wester, Brock and Little reported safe . . . LVT abandoned .*

*."...*they *will remain ashore tonight.* "

Dragging that water can was no easy job, and the barrage never let up. Sand, rock, chunks of concrete, boat and tank parts, truck engines, tires, helmets and bodies pelted us continuously. A Marine vanished in a multicolored explosion; body parts flying in all directions. His K-bar combat knife, whipped from its sheath, whirred like an angry hornet, corkscrewing through the air. It sliced off the tip of a crouching See-Bee's nose and laid open his cheek before burying its blade in the side of a crater beside a Marine, his ankle and foot dangling from an elongated strip of muscle tissue.

"Help me," he whispered. I splinted his ankle as best I could, using a bayonet sheath and a lot of wrapping.

One of our small 75mm howitzers fired into Suribachi, another fired at the airfield, and another blasted Hill 382 to our right. But they didn't seem to have much effect. I dragged the guy to the beach and laid him beside Margie June. I figured the

Japs knew the *LVT* was no longer a threat and would not waste ammo on it.

A commander, an older man, very calm and very brave, whose name I, unfortunately, do not remember other than it reminded me of a tobacco company, like P. Lorrilard or Phillip Morris or Reynolds, explained he was a doctor, that all his corpsmen were dead or missing, and asked if I could help him put together an aid station. Of course I could, and did.

[*Setting up with tobacco Doc*]

Tobacco Doc set up while I dragged the wounded in. We worked well together. I muscled the men onto stretchers or lay them on ponchos, whatever was available. The doc treated the worst cases first. This routine lasted about an hour. Finally a corpsman crawled in and immediately went to work. That corpsman was actually more help than I. Later a Jap in a nearby bunker shot him. It had been my job to check that bunker earlier. The enemy inside appeared dead when I cleared it. But one must have been unconscious or playing. At any rate, the Jap fired through the opening and killed the corpsman. I hated

The careful application of terror is also a form of communication

myself for not being more careful. Why hadn't I shot each one of the bodies just for safety's sake? Now it was too late. I dumped a grenade in the hole and blew the whole bunch to hell.

Later another medic, Lt. Long barreled in to assist. By this time we had about eight or ten men awaiting attention, and about the same amount had already been treated. Explosions created huge craters and we soon had three in a row, which allowed us a fair-sized hospital area. We lined men on each side, with more arriving every minute. Both doctors worked like madmen trying to save our guys. Plasma flowed from bottles hung on upended rifles. We had stored bottles in folded stretchers for the makeshift triages. I saw a bundle of those stretchers float ashore, but before I could retrieve the bundle, a tank ran over it. The plasma seeped through the canvas and into the sand. A terrible waste.

Lt. Long woke me with his shouting. He pointed to an *LCVP*, unbroached and unhit; the ramp was down. Another work party strained with lines to the stern, fighting the surf. Evacuation for the wounded had arrived.

We transported injured men to the boat by any and every means. In spite of the pain, any walking wounded assisted one another and even carried the stretcher cases. We loaded as many as we could yet hundreds waited. This was one of the few boats that made it in and out that day.

Further down the beach, some tractors traded ammo for wounded. Stoney and the rest of my crew had made it out to the boats. Stoney's report read, in part, "... the last time I saw Corporal Marshall he crawled from the bunker, saying 'they needed help up front and was going up to kill some Japs' . . .."

The beach shut down at eleven pm that night; no way to get in or continue to evacuate the wounded. Captain Bill Connors persuaded an *LST* captain, mortar fire be damned, to keep the nose of his ship against the beach and not retreat out to sea as intended. They had supplies and we needed them. Meanwhile, Lt. Art Haas, our shore control officer, raced back and forth,

Alligator Marines

waving his arms guiding tractors loaded with vital materials off that ship to designated areas whenever possible.

D + 1, February 20, 1945

0600

"AJ to AB6. Check on number 93 . . . Howard is missing."

"AK to AC. Your man, D. B. Marshall, is working with the medical department of the Infantry."

"A42 to AD. What do you want us to do?"

"Do you have a load aboard?"

"Negative . . . we are empty . . . many tracs around us are out of action."

"AF to AJ. Need operator to replace Meoska."

"AB6 to AJ, Have lost four LVTs in explosion . . . some wounded . . . gas situation bad on Blue 2."

"AJ to Wheelock. Where are you?"

"On APA 193 . . . can't get off due to air raid."

"AJ to all units. All units report to Pooper on Blue 2 for assignment."

Unknown: "Oh crap, remember the Alamo . . . old Tex could die today . . . hot crap."

"AJ to all units. Cut out the crap on the radio . . . someone is always listening."

"To Gilstrom, Polack, Motyka and Paris . . . this is *Buffalo* . . . make sure your men and companies use proper radio procedure...You are responsible."

Chapter 26: There is absolutely no substitute for the lack of preparation

In time, other corpsmen and bandsmen showed up to take my place. I explained to Tobacco Doc how I arrived in the first place and he permitted me to continue my mission. As Doc thanked me, I took off with the original water can. En route, I picked up a 12-gauge pump shotgun and joined the unit. A different sergeant was now in charge and other faces had joined the crew. They received the water most gratefully.

The enemy, as tenacious as ever; concealed themselves in pillboxes that resembled evil-eyed crocodiles winking an incessant stream of death. "If you can't see them," the sergeant yelled, "bend up their fucking gun muzzles, bend up them fucking muzzles— shoot, shoot, shoot!"

During this time, our tractor men worked like dogs, trying to keep the invasion on schedule.

"AJ to all units. What are LVT . . . [garbled]?"

Unknown: "Damned if I know ... will find out and send them to the beach."

"Bl to AJ. Number 57 is finally running . . . having motor trouble."

"AJ to Bl. Get him to the beach as soon as possible."

"AJ to all units. LSTs 713, 731, 789 and 684 can take LVTs for reloading . . . also need gasoline pumps on Blue 2."

"AF to AJ. LVTs 17 and 20 crews safe. "

"A to AJ. LVTs 76 and 78 aboard 1ST 787 , , , all OK . .. C 84 is on 787 . . . Rayniak, Tallant, Wood and Tacoma all OK. "

"AJ to AMI. Why is LST drifting to right . . . have him come left."

"AMI to AJ. LST having steering problems."

"AJ to AD. Send Thomas ashore . . . need telephone lines set up."

Unknown: *"Who in hell is he going to call?"*

"AB6 to A. Oprisko has relieved Meoska." "AMI to AJ. Top sergeant and Tommy request to go ashore."

"AJ to AMI. Permission denied."

Continuously keeping up the fire into the pillboxes, one or two men crawled up the openings and tossed in explosives. Some squads had flame-throwers. The whooshing, cracking sound of the flame appeased us, yet they were so distant. It seemed that, in our sector, we fought one pile of rubble after another, and each pile fought back.

These combat squads had trained together on Maui and the big island of Hawaii, and each man knew the other and his capabilities. They had us firing lots of slugs to keep the Japs pinned down. I preferred grenades, but they were at a premium, and these squads knew what they were doing, anyway. As stated before, a Marine is, first and foremost, a rifleman, so I pumped away with the shotgun, knowing that each round sent nine double "0" .32-caliber slugs into Jap gun ports.

Daisy cutters, flat trajectory fire, had been the biggest worry, but now mortars rumbled and grumbled closer. The combination of hot lead and steel was so concentrated in our direction, that one guy claimed he could light a cigarette just by holding it above ground level.

A close hit jostled our hole; we clawed for the bottom. Another burst closer . . . and another. The battery thundered overhead. Two men died, several more wounded. Dirt and debris showered us. We bounced up to resume fire, but I found a sliver of mortar penetrating the breech of my 12-gage and it jammed. I tossed it and banged away with my .45 pistol, a worthless effort at 20 yards, but it made noise.

Someone yelled, "*Marshall get more grenades*!" I crawled out and found a ditch full of wounded and dead Marines near the edge of the airfield. Most of them had grenades on their belts. Filling a gas mask bag, I dragged it, along with some bandoleers of Ml ammo. They needed *more* grenades. There had to be some somewhere. Back to the beach, I went.

Getting away from that hell-fire beach

Along the route, I found a Thompson submachine gun, dirty but operable. Someone had stenciled BP on the stock, meaning Beach Party, I suppose. Slinging the strap over my shoulder I headed for the terrace. A work party of about 30 men lined up, passing boxes from a landing craft. Approaching to ask about grenades, a shell screamed in and the group disappeared in a massive explosion.

I flew up and back probably 20 feet. It knocked the wind out of me burying my face in the sand. Trying desperately to suck air into my lungs, I succeeded only in getting a throat full of black sand. Coughing, gagging and weeping, I floundered around, unaware of my surroundings or the situation. A hand grabbed my shoulder strap and yanked me, still gasping, to my feet. Little remained of the work party. Arms, legs and torsos lay strewn about. Not a whole body remained in the entire group.

Tears streamed down my face. I coughed up sand, choked and blubbered at the same time. Funny words dropped from my mouth. I felt someone pushing me into the landing craft; I didn't resist.

The boat bobbed in the surf. While steadying myself, crewmen dragged other wounded up the ramp. More shells came in. The ramp had to be raised quickly. Shells bracketed the boat and one of the four wounded tumbled over the side. With the ramp raised, our coxswain maneuvered the craft into a turn. We took two hits— one through the hull; the other just missed the helmsman but hit the engine room.

The shot-up hull took in water and the throttle then jammed at low speed. The rudder wedged itself tight at a slight angle. For the hits we took, overall damage didn't seem too bad. The crew kept the engine running to keep the bilge pumps operating. We chugged onward, making a large, lazy arc away from that hell-fire beach heading in a northerly direction. We waved and hollered, to no avail. Ships, landing craft and amphibious tractors charging back and forth were far too busy to take notice of our puny, disabled craft.

"AJ to all units. Missing tracs are 58, 39f 57, 42 and 37 ... look for them and if located . . . get them aboard for the present time."

"Al to AJ. Am taking 2nd Armored aboard ... am *sending Pizella ashore with gas and* ammo."

"AB6 to AJ. Numbers 60 and 80 beyond repair . . . 36 flooded . . . 97 internal drive sheared . . . 48 down. .. 64 is working on 47, 94 and 66 but believe they are beyond repair . . . also 51 is down."

"AMI to AJ. A7 hit by fire . . . all dead . . . B32 ramp broke ... [unintelligible] . . . motor out . . . B31 went to beach for repair . . . hit by fire on way in ... bilge pumps out . . . unknown LVT sunk by LST . . . B33 bilge pumps out . . . motor gone . . . sunk before reaching LVT . . . A3 sank on way to LVT."

Oblivious to all this carnage, I finally came to my senses, coughed up and spit out the last of the black sand.

"Where ya headed?" I asked, "I need to get to *LST 764* or to *789.*" The Navy guys thought it a great idea but impossible to do with no tools to free the rudder. We were all in the same boat and had only one option, to attract attention and get a tow.

We bumbled about halfway through the apogee of our arc, still heading northward when night fell. Our curving course slowly angled us back toward that damned island. The engine had to be kept running to work the pumps; it also kept the prop

Absolutely no substitute

turning because the linkage was jammed. The angled rudder guided us ever closer to shore.

In the failing light, we could feel the water sloshing about our ankles; the bilge pump couldn't keep up.

Remembering our briefing of Iwo Jima's topography and what could be seen by the shell flashes, I estimated that we would be ashore somewhere above the jutting, rocky northeast tip of the pork-chop-shaped island.

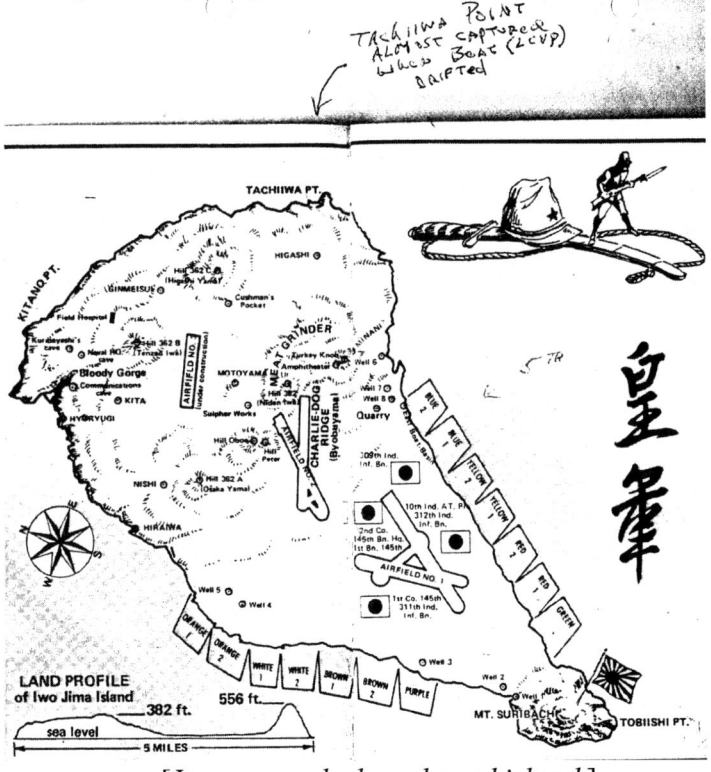

[*It was a pork chop shaped island.*]

As clouds invaded the sky, the weather, combined with sea spray, turned icy cold. The ocean went black. Even though we bobbed between the island and our battle wagons, we were more alone than ever. Every time a ship's huge guns belched fire, we cheered. Sometimes we caught glimpses of red-hot shells arching overhead. We hoped each and every one reached its target. Our elation died quickly via the light from a parachute flare almost directly over our heads.

We recognized it as Japanese by its greenish tint. The brilliant glare also revealed how dangerously close we drifted to the rocky shore. Much to our discomfort, we clearly caught sight of an enemy patrol crawling around and over the shore rocks in the direction we floated. The Japanese must have thought we were a landing party or something.

In reality, we were sitting ducks on display like in a Macy's store window at Christmas. Had they known our true situation, those soldiers would have laughed themselves silly.

The flare hissed out. With limited options, we considered turning off the engine to halt our progress but that meant stopping the pump, and we'd sink. Yet, as long as the screw turned, it was certain we would be delivered to the waiting Japanese. The two Navy boys frantically hammered on the controls in the engine room. Their efforts proved useless.

As they emerged, covered with sweat, grease and bilge oil, another flare burst with a hollow, popping sound. One of the men held a flashlight; I suggested he use it to signal the ships that were lobbing shells over our heads. Maybe, just maybe, one of them might get curious and attempt a rescue. The flashlight barely threw a beam; its batteries were exhausted, nevertheless, the swabbie raised it over the gunnel, aimed toward our fleet and blinked out dot-dot-dot, dash-dash-dash, dot-dot-dot, SOS, the only Morse signal any of us knew.

A few minutes later, another enemy flare illuminated the shore. Good grief! The shore was now only a few hundred feet away. The enemy patrol waited; we could actually see the men conversing. We presented easy targets, but they didn't fire. They wanted prisoners. I knew once the interrogation was over we would be butchered. No Marine taken prisoner in the islands was ever found alive.

Men of the 5th Amphs were being butchered, too.

"AB6 to AJ. Any report on 'C' Company maintenance and men....have been missing for some time."

"No report as yet."

"A to AJ. Tractors that have been sunk are 15, 14,25, 18, 65, 67, 14, 89, 70, 69, Al, 45, 49, 55, 58, 52, AC75, 77, 19, 82, 92, 91, 89, AMI, 32, 31, 3, 33."

Unknown. "71 *not sunk, is aboard LST 76 Improbably mistaken for 77.*"

"AJ to all units. Where is Blackjack?......... No answer was made."

"AJ to AC. Get all tractors dispatched to beach........ .Now goddamnit. . . I said move them now!"

"AC to AJ. Roger."

"Pooper to AJ. I have LVT 48 crew on the beach in bomb crater."

Clutching my Thompson and patting my .45; it appeared only I was armed on board. And I would go down hard. Yet, another flare offered a glimmer of hope. Again remembering that pork chop map, the flare revealed that we bobbed about a mile and a half north of our gang on Blue Beach 2. I thought if we could kill every Jap in that patrol, avoid the high cliff behind and crawl or swim through the surf (avoiding sharks, which, with our luck, were getting ready for dinner) then sneak past the rock quarry and through the East Boat Basin, we would be within our own lines, maybe. It was a dumb idea at best, but....I patted the 45 again.

By the fifth or sixth flare, we could see a ground swell had us by the balls. The Japs waved and laughed. The flare hissed out. We kept bob-bob-bobbing along. I pulled the bolt on the Thompson. Island-ripping salvos screamed overhead.

Then our engine gurgled and died.

Dumb dumb dumb *dumb*, I thought.

Someone on our Ark heard the thrumming of an engine. We listened; we couldn't see in the pitch black. One of the men whispered, "It's ours; they're coming to get us."

"Like hell they are," I growled. "Those are Japs."

Out of the gloom a voice called, "Hey, you guys, where the hell are you?"

I, of course, knew the Japs were setting us up and warned, "Don't answer 'em. It's a trick."

Caught in the ground swell and sinking, we waited in silence. Ha, they'd play hell getting me!

Again, out of the gloom, a voice growled, "Well, fuck 'em. If they don't want to get picked up, let's get the hell out of here."

That had to be our Navy! Everyone in our boat yelled. Me, too.

The *LCM* (Landing Craft Mechanized, twice the size of our Higgins boat) churned in, bumped us hard, gave us a towline and backed rapidly out to sea. The rescue crew— I think they were Coast Guard men— hauled us aboard, soaked but safe. They cut the line to our swamped *LCVP*, and we motored off. From a distance, we watched another flare drift down, this time illuminating a broad, empty expanse of dark water. Did the Japanese ever figure out if we sank or were saved?

The *LCM* crew told us it was the Japanese flares and not our feeble SOS signals that alerted the battle fleet that something was amiss. Only by accident had some sharp-eyed crewman spotted our little, broken-down craft bobbing in an unauthorized area off the enemy shore.

The radio crackled out an air raid warning

Shivering uncontrollably from our close call, a rising wind and stinging rain, we presented a logistical problem to our rescuers. While they were deciding where to deliver us, the radio crackled out an air raid warning. Immediate fleet blackout prevailed. Ships, dropping smoke pots off the fantails, scattered in every direction. Again, we were where we shouldn't be ... in the middle of an invasion fleet desperately avoiding Japanese bombers.

In real danger of being run down, no one would have noticed or cared if we had. For the next four or five hours every one of us lived in absolute terror. Our coxswain cursed and shouted as we rocked and dodged huge black, engine-thumping monsters, each thundering out of nowhere and lit up only by the ack-ack bursts, passing close enough to fling us aside and throw us whirling in their wake.

The carrier *Bismarck Sea* was lost in that raid. Several ships were hit, and all 50 of the Kamikaze raiders were shot down.

At long last, our rescuers contacted an *APA*, the *Bayfield*, and transferred us aboard. The *Bayfield's* crew crowded around. "How we doin'?" I didn't have much of an answer. "It's pretty tough but we're makin it." A doctor tended my minor wounds. "How we doin?" I gave him the same answer. The other Marines were hurt worse than I. Hot coffee and a bottle of brandy put me at ease, and a helpful corpsman led me to a sack. I refused to give up my Thompson until a Marine guard guaranteed me he would watch over it. To his query I gave a somewhat different answer, "We're getting the shit kicked out of us. *But we got the airfield.*"

Five hours later, my eyes opened. A different guard stood duty. With a wide grin he handed over my newly cleaned and oiled weapon. It was almost unrecognizable as the rusty piece I had earlier relinquished.

[*Litter on the beach*[

Chapter 27: Someone who thinks logically is a nice contrast to the real world

D + 2, February 21, 1945

0540 hours

"A6 to AJ. Need 80mm ammo and gas . . . also send Andy in to Pooper."

"AMI to AJ. Number 93 sunk . . . crew safe."

"Al to AJ. Loaded with rations . . . going to beach."

"AB6 to AJ. Number 80 is hit . . . heavy damage . . . two wounded."

"AJ to AL. Where is OVT 64?"

"A6 to AJ. Rations will be scattered on the beach."

"A to AJ. Pooper is OK . .. Andy aboard Mica . . . "C" Company maintenance destroyed."

"AB6 to AJ. Have two tractors down . . . four disabled ... or demolished . . . seven are repairable."

"AMI to AJ. An LVT will report to you . . . belongs to 10th Amph Trac . . . he is lost . . . keep him and use him."

"AJ to all units. Need muster roll of living and dead."

"AD to AJ. Am loading 10th Amph Trac . . . what do you need?"

"AJ to AD. Need mortar, small arms . . . water . . . heavy demolition . . . get it here soon as possible."

"AC to AJ. We are moving further out to sea . . . skipper of Mica says condition red . . . can you read me . . . we are fading."

Unknown: "Maybe you are going to Hawaii . . . say hello to the girls."

"All units . . . cut out the crap."

I emerged topside of the *Bayfield* and immediately headed toward a Marine peering intently through binoculars at the devastation on shore. Tapping him on the shoulder, I asked if he knew where one could catch a boat back to the beach.

"Why?" He asked mystified. I explained about mistakenly being shuffled off the island and needed to get back to my outfit; barring that, I'd join up with another.

Two hard objects dug into my back—the muzzles of two Thompsons, held by General Clifton B. Gates' personal bodyguards. It was the general himself I had so brashly approached!

Good God, how else could I screw up?

The general made a written notation of my name and unit, motioned to a near-by runner and ordered me to stand by.

The *APA* was a beehive of activity. A constant stream of boats flowed back and forth, transporting wounded and taking back messages and supplies. I waited unobtrusively, hoping the general wouldn't have me shot or something.

The runner returned and spoke to the general, who then motioned to me. He ordered me to go with the runner; a boat waited and, "... for God's sake get rid of that white shirt."

A one-man invasion of Iwo Jima

After scrambling down the cargo net to an *LCVP* manned by a crewman and coxswain, we roared away.

"Where to?"

"The beach."

"The beach?"

Both men turned toward the beach. It was covered with burning, exploding wreckage. They stared; only an idiot would voluntarily return to that inferno.

"Oh, Gawd!" one of them moaned, expressing the sentiments of both.

Neither seemed happy about his new assignment, but, if General Gates ordered it, then this nut must be vitally important for some reason and, come hell or high water, they'd get him ashore.

My feelings reflected theirs and, for the first time, I felt I was a tremendously important Marine and rose admirably to the occasion.

The beach lay in waste as far as one could see. It contained a sloshing mass of torn bodies, clothing, paper, photographs, tins and boxes of food, stretchers, life rafts and wrecked landing craft along with half-buried tanks, big guns and tractors. As we drew closer, I instructed the crewman to lower the ramp only part way, just enough for me to make it over the top so they could back off as quickly as possible. We snaked between the wreckage. There were no wounded where we came in, only dead. I rushed up the ramp and leaped off. Thus, I made a one-man invasion of Iwo Jima. The boat backed off.

[*The beach lay in waste...*]

I recognized *Eagan's* tractor there. A shell-torn jeep hung from the ramp and a large hole gapped in the underbelly of the tractor near the cab. No bodies, no blood. Whew.

The sailors who brought me in were now in trouble. Their boat lurched in the surf directly in front of an approaching tractor. The driver of the tractor pulled his left brake in an attempt to turn. It was no use; the monster ground up and over the foundering boat. Plywood sides splintered under the terrific weight and riped open track growsers. My seamen chauffeurs dove frantically into the debris-filled water. I hoped they made it.

Amid the overwhelming oder of salt air mingled with explosives and rotten flesh, I gathered grenades from the rubble to take back to the 25th. Scrambling up the terrace, I hoped to keep up with some tanks moving forward. On the way, I looked for those mortar clinics and Tobacco Doc. I couldn't even find the big holes we had set up in. Artillery fire had changed everything and everyone in the aid station was dead. Japanese Colonel Chosaku Kaido, Chief of Artillery, did his murderous work well.

As a mortar crew set up their tube, I asked, "Can I help?" They said yes, they would appreciate it, and directed me to set up sighting markers. They handed me several metal rods from cloverleaf ammo containers. My job was to crawl out and jam the rods in the ground where they directed. When I got back, they had the mortar in position and were dropping in rounds. After the third or fourth shot, one of the men broke out a bottle of Four Roses whiskey and, in appreciation of my services, offered me a drink. They never slowed their pace, arming and sighting, even when the bottle passed around. I joked about dropping the bottle down the tube instead of a round.

"Never happen," they hollered. We laughed.

Finishing a cigarette, I thanked them and fell in behind some tanks. The tanks crawled up to the airfield, by-passing several of the positions we had knocked out the day before. These places always presented a danger. Tunnels, constructed by the *204th Naval Construction Battalion* allowed snipers access to our rear and flanks. Wreckage pushed from the airfield, a discarded box or blanket rag, and, in some places, even the natural shadow of a rock or bank could be one of these concealed rifle ports. If possible, they advised us to lie quiet and hold fire until we spotted a slight movement.

Moving inland, a number of us crouched behind the tanks. A gun port popped to life on our right. The shell missed the tank and sailed over our heads toward the beach. I made a dash for the telephone on the back of the Sherman, but another Marine saw the Jap gun at the same time I did. He got on the phone and gave directions, the turret swung and the gunner made a perfect hit.

Kuribayashi's *Prowling Wolves*

Days and nights ran together in a blur of explosions and zinging bullets. I found a Marine buddy, Pvt. Thurman Mott, and shared his hole for a night. One man to a hole invited certain death or capture. We shared K rations and bedded down below the cold wind and rain. The bottom of the hole radiated heat from Iwo's active volcano. We could hear what we thought was hot lava flowing below. Some of the guys thought it might be Jap tunnelers. Not really knowing or caring; the warmth felt good.

Try as we might, neither of us could keep our eyes open. Breaking though a foggy sleep, squeezing fingers at my throat jolted me awake. A Jap straddled my chest! He was one of Kuribayashi's *Prowling Wolves,* a group of volunteers who gathered intelligence by probing our lines and quietly taking prisoners. His leg blocked the holster of my .45. Unable to break his grip on my neck, in desperation, I forced both knees up and slammed him in the rump. The unexpected blow catapulted him over my head. I seized my pistol, rolled and took aim, but the prowling wolf had vanished in the dark. Mott slept soundly on.

"AB to *AJ. B31 bilge pump out . . . B32 ramp broke . . . 33 bilge out . . . A14 is full of holes and A 15 has been rammed. The following day we approached another LCI."*

"AJ to AD. When can you take tracs aboard?"

"About an hour."

"Why so long?"

"LST ramp broke."

"Hurry up, dammit. "

"AJ to all units. Get water and ammo to the beach . . .

"AC to AJ. Unable to launch tractors . . . moving out to sea . . . have to load 5-inch shells on a tin can."

Unknown: *"AC is going to make it to Hawaii yet."*

"AJ to LST 787. Get bow doors open . . . get to beach and unload!"

[*Get back to the beach and unload*]

Someone who thinks logically is a nice contrast to the real world

"787. We are doing the best we can . . . Skipper says there are mines on the beach . . . we are under heavy fire."

Unknown: "No *mines on beach . .. we are having a picnic here on Blue 2 . . . send in the food.". . . we are under heavy mortar fire .... keep tracs off the beach!"

"AJ to Al. Any info on 52 or 55?"

"Negative."

"AJ to Al. Have authority to unload ships."

"AJ to B6. LST 787 is on Yellow beach . . . they have gas and oil . . . it is up to you to get it . . . get report on all LVTs that are serviceable."

"AC to J. Number 99 is out here . . . dead but afloat."

"Al to AM. Number 59 needs small boat to take off crew. . . it is sinking.

Time 1540

"All units, Condition Red! Condition Red!"

Unknown: "Right on, Marines . . . it is a good day to die."

"Al to AJ. Any news of 44 or 48? . . . They were headed to the beach."

"Negative."

"AMI to all units. We will keep working tonight as much as possible."

"AB6 to AJ. Number 52 is out of gas . . . 53 is running but in bad shape."

"AK to AJ. There are three tractors burning on beach. . . we are under heavy mortar fire .... keep tracs off the beach!"

"AJ to Al. Any info on 52 or 55?"

"Negative."

"AJ to Al. Have authority to unload ships."

Alligator Marines

"AJ to B6. LST 787 is on Yellow beach . . . they have gas and oil . . . it is up to you to get it . . . get report on all LVTs that are serviceable."

"AC to J. Number 99 is out here . . . dead but afloat." "Al to AM. Number 59 needs small boat to take off crew. . . it is sinking.

Someone who thinks logically is a nice contrast to the real world

Chapter 28: Friends may come and friends may go, but enemies accumulate

Word passed around we had lost 2,500 men the first day. I believed it. One battalion lost nineteen officers with their entire command post wiped out. I believed that, too!

Such news crushed the men *and* it increased our determination.

Tanks and tractors clanked forward, inviting a storm of unwelcome fire, but also carried welcomed supplies of ammo, water, and food. Some of the food was even hot! Once unloaded though, we wished those tractors were someplace else.

About the fourth day after landing, while in a rear guard position at the airfield, I ran into my buddy Eagan. "By God, you're not *dead*! They reported you dead!" he exclaimed elated. The elation quickly took a back seat to war-ridden diligence. Behind us, enemy snipers took occasional shots. Above, a Marine Corsair swooped down in a brutal strafing run. The speeding line of tracers came directly for *us!* Shit. We dove for cover. The spray of bullets missed. Those damned Japs had sneaked the colored, front-line marking strips to our rear. The Marine pilot had no idea.

"The flag! The flag!"

As we moved, we popped away at the re-occupied bunkers, Eagan with his M-1 and I with the Thompson. Behind us, a Marine, wildly yelling and waving his arms, bolted straight for us. We hunkered down preparing for the worst; his frantic signaling must be warning of an attack from the rear. As he closed in, we just made out his words, "The flag! The flag!" At the same time, he motioned toward the mountain.

Barely discernible, the stripes fluttered on the crest. *Our Flag*! Our ranks slowed their fire and began cheering. Hundreds of ships set up a cacophony of shrill whistles. It was pure music to our ears. We had the mountain. Goddamn, we actually had Suribachi!!

[*Eagan and me in foxhole when Marine was shouting and pointing that the flag was being raised.*]

Infuriating the Japs, their fire increased ten-fold along with our resolve. The 3rd Division was now ashore, they were to push up the island's center. The 5th continued fighting on the west side, as did the 4th on the east. I stayed with the 4th and alternated between the 23rd and the 25th. It was impossible to keep track of units or know their situation.

Charley Dog ridge

All night, every night, swinging parachute flares animated the living and dead. Artillery kept up a reign of terror, sparing nothing. Someone shoved a walkie-talkie in my hands, and we were told to get a .30-caliber machine gun and take a position on Charley Dog ridge.

Even here the Japanese, sent out *Prowling Wolves,* unarmed, no helmets or any item that would make noise. An unwary marine would be muffled, knocked unconscious and dragged into a tunnel for interrogation before being brutally killed. The only orders *we* had were, "Don't shoot any of our men but blow the hell out of anything else that moves!"

Every half-hour we awaited the signal from the first outpost in a line of six, a whispered, "Charley Dog One," meaning the first outpost on the ridge was okay. Immediately, "Charley Dog Two," followed meaning the second outpost was alert and not overrun. Each post followed in numerical order until the last post on the eastern edge of the ridge finished with "Charley Dog Six." Any omission in the sequence meant that post had been overrun and there was now a hole in the line.

We mounted our machine gun, as best we could, on the edge of a crater, putting some rocks and discarded tank tracks around it as protection. Ege and I sat back and waited. We had been told to expect a patrol through our area. We managed to stay awake the first half of the night, straining our eyes past the swinging shadows. Then, sure enough, I elbowed my partner to confirm a movement in a ditch about 10 yards to our front. He swung the barrel of the gun in that direction.

At that moment the call "Charley Dog One" came low over the walkie-talkie; "Charley Dog Two" answered on cue. I whispered my call, "Charley Dog Three," and added that we had movement to our front. The operator reminded me of the expected patrol. Four, Five, then Six answered in sequence.

We watched. Soon a voice called out from the ditch, "Minneapolis." Okay. Our password that night was any American city except Chicago. Other nights, it might be any American automobile except Ford or any tree except palm, simple enough and very effective if you got the word. I answered with "Los Angeles." The voice returned, "We're coming in." Another flare stalled them momentarily, but soon the soldiers crawled, exhausted, into our hole. What a relief!

Alligator Marines

After resting, they bellied on to make their report. Again, Ege and I were alone. Exhausted, we dropped off and missed the next call. They sent a patrol to see if we had been compromised. Just as they scuffled up from behind, I jolted awake. Banging the walkie-talkie, I cussed as if it weren't working. The ruse worked. They returned to command and reported that all was well, just a defective radio unit. Whew; I would have hated to be caught asleep, by *either side*.

Fifth Amph radio log D + 3, February 22, 1945

0700, watch begins.

"AF to AJ. Tractors sunk are 75, 77, 79, 82, 92, 99, 17 and 20."

"AI to AJ. Number 45 sunk, 49 engine dead, 55 final drive sheared, 58 sunk after being hit by small arms, 52 sunk by leaking ramp."

"AB6 to AJ. Too many tracs on beach . . . too bunched up."

"AC to J. We are moving out to sea . . . can you read me?"

Unknown: "Who cares?"

"AJ to AB6. Report one of our tracs is on Red Beach 1. What is it doing there?"

"AB6 to AJ. Do not know , . . will try to check."

"AJ to all units. All men not accounted for should be listed as missing."

"AMI to AJ. Number 59 engine out."

"AMI to AJ. LVT nearby has broken ramp."

"AMI to AF. Crew of 29 aboard LST 731 ... Gallagher, Jennings and Barr."

to "AI to AJ. Number 96 crew safe aboard LST 763."

"AB6 to AJ. Tracs ashore are 36, 73, 8, 52, 77, 42, 41, 38, 55 and 61."

Someone who thinks logically is a nice contrast to the real world

"AB6 to AJ. Heed report on Ross, Hagedorn, Smith and Mullen . . . they are missing."

"Al to AJ. Baldyf Felice and Buffalo have gone ashore."

"AJ to Al. Why did Baldy go ashore? He was supposed stay aboard the Mica."

Unknown: "To get a haircut, damn it ... why do you think?!"

"This is AJ. Astonish. Who is this? I'll court martial you for this transmission. All units . . . cut the crap on the air!"

"AB4 to AD. Any news of B13?"

"Negative."

"AMI to AJ. Number 59 is along side 1ST 731 . . . engine out from small arms fire and one big hit . . . crew safe."

"AD to AJ. Condition Red . . . air raid . . . air raid ... no LVTs can be loaded or unloaded."

"AJ to AD. My ass really bleeds for you. Take them aboard."

Back on D day, when the first waves approached the beach, one of General Kuribayashi's radio operators deep within his bunker somehow got onto our radio frequency. The general himself had a few words to say to the landing force.

The general spoke excellent English. "*Marines, we are about to engage in a great battle, the outcome of which will be a crushing victory for the Imperial Japanese forces. It is unfortunate that so many brave men shall die. We now give the final measure of loyalty, and the victory will be decided by the bravest.*"

Several of our tractor men heard this and wondered just who the speaker was and where he got so much confidence.

Of the 400 tractors comprising elements of the 5th, 10th, 3rd and 11th Amphibious Battalions involved in landing and supply, an estimated 133 had already been lost. Three days of relentless carnage began to tell on the exhausted Marines. Tempers flared.

The high loss of equipment and phenomenal number of casualties in so short a time appalled all. We constantly screamed for artillery;. 37's and 75 mm were ineffective. Twelve 105's had been pre-loaded aboard *DUKWs* and were en route. Eight suffered engine failures and sank. Gun power and crew power, all gone. Two more *DUKWs* broached in the heavy surf dumping their precious cargo into the sucking black sand. Finally we managed to haul two ashore but it took hours dragging heavy pieces into firing position. Only two out of twelve made it, but it was something.

The general had made his point.

Exhausted men didn't think clearly. Cpl. Bruno Laurenti cursed mightily when the captain of an *LST* refused to give the order to open the ship doors so amphibs could board. The result was that the amphib ran out of gas and drifted out to sea. Laurenti, Bill Seward and Al Hebert were elated when, two days later, a destroyer found them drifting some fifty miles closer to Tokyo than they meant to be. The tractor, named *Mama's Bathtub,* went under a short time later.

"*AD to AJ. Ship moving . . . ship won't stop.*"

"*AI to AC. Number 75 sunk . . . crew safe . . . 99 sighted ... 13 trying to get aboard LST.*"

"*96 to AJ. Numbers 95 and 99 aboard . . . all personnel OK.*"

"*AJ to all units. Unloading will continue through the night . . get gas and watch for control boat on way to beach . . . will have blue light on mast.*"

Unknown: "*This is Alley Cat. Marines don't recognize blue lights, only red ones.*"

"*All units. Cut out the garbage.*"

"*AD to AJ. Any reports on numbers 2f 5, 6, or 9?*"

"*Negative.*"

Someone who thinks logically is a nice contrast to the real world

"AD to AJ. Pizelli is missing . . . Oprisko on beach radio now."

"A1 to AJ. Where the hell is Nuzzo?"

"AJ to A1. Aboard Mica."

"AB6 to AJ. Number 47 is on beach, no crew."

"AJ to AC. Where is Paris? Get him over here. Stallings is wounded . . . need help."

"AJ to AC. Negative on last transmission . . . Stallings still on duty . . . being treated . . . does not need hospitalization."

"AJ to A, Any word on number 87?"

"Negative."

"AC to AJ. Check on Prorak and Pizella."

"AJ to AC. Prorak is OK . . . Pizella is missing."

"AD to AF. Number A18 crew safe . . . LVT sunk. Toth is missing . . . ashore some place."

"All units, Condition Red . . . Condition Red . . . keep working."

"AD to AB1. Send Hogan to beach . . . report to Pooper. . . Oprisko needs help."

"AJ to A1. Need tractor immediately on Blue 2 for critical work . . . send . . . send . . . send."

"A1 to AJ. Don't get your water hot. . . will send one."

[*Snipers and infiltrators constantly plagued our outpost*[

Chapter 29: By the time you make both ends meet, they move the ends

Making my way back to the beach on a warm sunny day, I passed the same crater where the mortar crew had set up. Mortar lay smashed and hurled about beside the bodies of the four soldiers I laughed and drank with a few days before. I think of them often.

Further on, I met up with an acquaintance from boot camp, Glen Pyle, a Texan. I needed water. Exchanging bits of news, he offered me his canteen. A sniper's bullet blasted it from his hand; the same bullet slicing the handle off my GI spoon. I tucked the bowl of the spoon into my breast pocket, which would accompany me for the rest of the campaign, and promptly fell asleep.

Awaking hours later with a sun-dried face and cracked lips, I bid Glen goodbye and headed out.

"*AJ to A1. Are you pulling out or going to a new position?*"

"*Al to AJ. I don't know........... the skipper won't talk to me.*"

"*AB6 to AJ. Need mechanics ashore we have moved.*"

"*AC to AD. No. 94 is out on Blue II...2 men aboard LST 789...there are four men aboard 94...where are other men?*"

"*AD to AC. They disappeared on the beach.*"

"*A92 to AC. We are 300 yards from you hold LST for us.*"

"*Baldy to AJ. I am ashore.*"

"*AG to AJ. Where are we to unload?*"

"*AJ to AG. See Pooper.*"

"*AK to AJ. Urgently need 3 doctors and corpsmen on Blue II*"

"AK to AJ. Two LVT's on beach numbers not readable."

"Al to AJ. Our skipper has orders to pull out at sunset".

"AJ to All Units. Stay on beach at sunset!"

"AC to AJ. LVT coining to us skipper will not open bow doors."

Unknown. *"Go to bridge to see skipper and take a .45 and reason with him and then maybe he will listen to you."*

"All units...cut out the crap."

"AC to AJ. Our skipper is staying to pick up strays"

Unknown. *"The system works every time...the .45 system."*

One memorable incident occurred as our tractors still caught hell. An ammo dump blew up in a horrific explosion. In spite of the danger, Charley Willoughby charged through the inferno, jumped into a stalled tractor and drove it safely out. "We needed it," was his only comment.

D + 4 0600 watch begins.

"AJ to AK. Some of our tractors are on Yellow Beach. Correct this."

"92 to AC. What is your location?"

"AC to 92. Near LST 787 and 812."

"A80 to AJ. Where is LST 764?"

"AJ to A80. Astern of us near LST 930 which is the hospital ship."

"AJ to AC. Check all intercom boxes... some transmission on the air that should not be."

"A to AC. Number 75 has a sheared final drive . . . will tow to beach and unload cargo."

"AC to AJ. A "B" Company tractor . . . number not readable, is sinking 2200 yards from beach."

"80 to AC. Number 73 will take cargo to beach."

"AJ to Al. Send only tracs to the beach that can get back by 1700 hours . . .also need casualty report."

"AD4 to AJ. Waiting to go on Mica . . . how long must we wait?"

"AJ to AD4. Don't know."

"AD4 to AJ. Better find out . . . we are sinking."

"Al to AJ. What is priority on beach?"

"AJ to Al. Water . . . small arms . . . artillery ammo . . .as much as you can get."

"AJ to B6. No towing tracs to sea . . . they might sink."

"Al to AD. Have men from tracs 60, 61, 94 on our LST . . . will send them to Mica as soon as transport can be arranged."

"AB4 to AD. How much gas do you have?"

"AD to AB4. About 35 gallons in the tanks."

"AB4 to AD. I need gas!"

"AD to AB4. We don't have any cans to transfer."

"AB4 to AD. We are sinking ... we have wounded. They can't swim"

D + 5, February 24, 1945

"AJ to all units. All units move ashore . . . all tracs and equipment on Mica will be removed . . . everyone get to beach . . . command posts will be set up under direction of Baldy ... make all reports to beach . . . all units move to beach . . . if tracs unable to move from Mica . . . leave them . . . take all machine guns and ammo from disabled tractors to the beach . . . this is AJ, out."

Our initial projected four day operation before the 'big one' had now come to an end. Little equipment remained.

Word came up the line that 5th Amphs had established a command post on the beach. It was time to rejoin them. I finally found our group near the quarry at Blue 1. Though our machines had suffered a high attrition rate, luckily not many of our guys were killed or wounded. As a result, we now had more drivers and crewmen than tractors. This enabled us to supplement the ranks of the forward units, which I had been doing anyway.

There had been some question as to my being A.W.0.L

"Where in the God damn hell would I go to on this god damned island?" I checked in with Lts. Reece and Malcolm and submitted the written confirmation of my whereabouts in the last five days.

We set up light housekeeping and Samson joined us

Bob Hoover, Eagan, Diditch, Stan Gienko and Blyleven and I were ordered to establish a perimeter north of our CP. There were six derelict Japanese *LSMs* and cargo ships in the boat basin north of Blue 2. We selected one of the ships lying at right angles to the beach, a sort of steel wall. A .30-caliber mounted on the deck, buffered with some sand bags, gave us an ideal position and a pretty good view of the shore toward Tachiiwa Point, where my shipwreck companions and I had so narrowly escaped capture.

We set up light housekeeping in the ship's interior. Loads of volcanic ash provided fairly soft sleeping accommodations. Even our dog, Samson, moved in. A large volcanically hot shell hole in the sand alongside the ship contained constantly boiling water, perfect for washing our dirty clothes. A flat sheet of armor propped on the ship's deck made a great stove. In contrast to the last five days This was hog heaven for us.

We bedded down, changing guard every four hours. About midnight the first night, four Japs snuck within twenty feet of the boat. It was either Blyleven, or Samson, who spotted them.

Blyleven cranked off one round and his .30 jammed; he had forgotten to set the head space. It really didn't matter though, as one of the Japs panicked and detonated his own satchel charge. All four joined their ancestors.

Souvenir hunting bought rations

As usual, rations remained scarce. Souvenir hunting, though officially discouraged, provided a solution to those shortages. A type 99 Arisaka rifle traded to the Navy guys at the beach was worth four eggs or six potatoes. A 77. light machine gun "bought" us a gallon of 190-proof medicinal alcohol. Flags were exchanged for bread or canned meat. Once I got a gallon can with no label. I was amazed to find it contained beef and brown gravy. Beef and gravy in a can? Who knew? We had no such goodies during the Depression.

Other enemy articles were negotiable, but swords were the most valuable. Those of us aboard our private, beached yacht foraged daily when not on the line. Our ship soon earned a reputation for having all types of hot food, coffee (joe) and, when available, beer, pogey bait and liquor, all at no charge to members of the 5th Amphs.

I recall the time Major Shead escorted Admiral Raymond A. Spruance, USN, his chief of staff Admiral Davis, and their Marine guards aboard our "yatch." Johnny Shuflata fried potatoes off the flat plate of armor. "Welcome aboard, Admiral," chirped Johnny, extending a greasy paw for a handshake.

Major Shead cringed while the unabashed corporal continued, "... uh, I don't believe I know your friend." Admiral Spruance introduced his chief of staff. Johnny again extended his greasy paw. "Ah, yes, a good man, I've read about him. Would ya'all care for a cup of joe?"

Cups in hand, the delegation inspected our impromptu *Queen Mary*, then bid a cordial good-bye. Johnny, apparently unaware of his irreverence, responded, "It's been a pleasure, sir. Come back any time, sir." He paused, then added, "Yeah, and bring your friend, too."

Fifth Division men blasted their way up the island's west side. Third Division landed the third day and were blasting up the center, while Fourth moved north and east. They blasted their way past more than 5000 bunkers, pillboxes and tunnels. Our men above the quarry and along the Charlie Dog ridge came under heavy fire from some hidden position on East Beach. Blue 1 and 2 also took a steady pounding. Snipers and infiltrators constantly plagued our outpost, and one of our drivers, PFC Harry Mullins, while talking to buddies, let out a sigh and slumped to the ground. He had been shot through the head.

Skip Stalling had been wounded at the same time Engle got hit. While they carried a load of 105 ammo to the beach, a shell screamed in for a direct hit on their tractor. Skip suffered minor wounds and awoke to find Engle unconscious and bleeding badly. The explosion ripped Engle's helmet and dog tags from him. Someone found the items later in the wreckage and assumed Engle dead. But Skip had dragged him down to the water's edge where both were eventually evacuated.

Skip returned to the beach after being treated and was directed to run a message back to our *LST*. He jumped aboard an outgoing *LCVP* and while turning, it rammed an incoming *DUKW* (wheeled amphibian) loaded with Negro Army men. The bump was not severe, but one of their troops panicked and leapt over the side. Skip, in spite of his wounds, dove in after the man. The soldier, loaded with gear, quickly went under. Skip kicked down trying to reach the solider. He saw the man's eyes beseeching him as he sank. Stalling said he will always regret not being able to reach that solider.

Chapter 30: If it's stupid, but works, it ain't stupid

Because of general harassment and the death of Mullins, Lt. Malcolm asked me to try and take out the snipers in our immediate vicinity. Having a pretty good idea where they were holed up, I welcomed the mission. Northeast of our "yatch," sat four other Japanese wrecks, one of which lay parallel to the beach. The 4000 ton cargo ship had been beached during a storm and was not as heavily shell damaged as the other vessels. The Japanese built a small rail track to it unloading supplies with the aid of handcars. It seemed the most likely place to house snipers and our men on Hill 382, just north of us, had been complaining of snipers at their backs.

Dog-tired, men from the foxholes would not volunteer despite my coaxing. Finally I spotted George (Pete) Zarris. "Sure, Marshall. What the hell, why not?"

Pete and I crossed the open area between the wrecks and boarded the cargo ship from the low side. Once on deck, we listened carefully. We heard Japs moving inside and debated the best way to eliminate them. Pete spotted a shell hole high in the smoke stack. We knew the interior of the stack was accessible from the interior of the ship, and iron rungs would allow a man to station himself in the funnel at the hole. There, the enemy would have an open field of fire on our area and remain undetected.

Climbing the stack to drop grenades inside would expose us to other Japanese marksmen. Yet, to enter the ship, and be ambushed from the gangway, was suicide. We finally agreed that I would cover the main deck with my Thompson, while Pete scoured the beach debris for a can of gasoline. With pure luck, he succeeded and returned in about ten minutes, lugging a five-gallon can. We poured the can's entire contents down the open main hatch and watched it splash deck to deck. I tossed in a lighted torch.

Of course, we had no idea of the power of gasoline fumes, or fumes that may have accumulated from ruptured fuel tanks below. Either way, the deadly mixture exploded with one hell of a roar. The deck heaved and bellied up, throwing the two of us skyward a good ten feet. Flames shot from the hatch like an erupting volcano. Why we weren't thrown down that open hatch, I don't know. We staggered to our feet, running like hell for the railing and dove over.

The explosion rocked the whole area. Our guys in camp thought the Japs had pulled a suicide caper with us aboard. They figured us dead until the Pete and I emerged from the dense smoke. They explained how they picked off Japanese fleeing from the flames. Sniping from that location finally stopped. Afterwards, Pete Zarris and I laughed like hell at our narrow escape. Pete was a great guy.

That cargo ship burned for three days. Later Lt. Malcolm informed me that the heavy smoke forced some of our cruisers to change firing positions. They were *not* happy with me.

Behind enemy lines

On Sunday, I think, they ordered us to report to the 24th near Charlie Dog ridge, now a gateway to the heart of the island. There was supposed to be a little town there, but it remained unseen by us. The casualties near Charlie Dog were high; the C.O. had been killed, along with most of the officers. Squad leaders took a hell of a beating, and the ranks wore thin. When we reached the area, two tomato plants tempted us with two luscious, ripe tomatoes growing in the warmth of a fumarole. Walt, Monte Pfister and Bert Gustafson wouldn't touch them with a ten-foot pole; believing they were classical Japanese poisoned bait. Their reluctance suited me fine. I plopped down and savored both tomatoes. The island offered me a sweet moist gift and how could I refuse?

If it's stupid, but works, it ain't stupid

In this same area, not far from the tomato plant, I discovered a pair of the most elegant, soft, brown leather English riding boots. Although not an expert in this field, these appeared to be expensive and possibly booby trapped. Though I steered clear, the memory of such strange objects in the midst of a war-torn Pacific island remains to this day. On reflection, they certainly belonged to Lt. Col. (Baron) Takeischi Nishi, a superb horseman, 1932 Olympic gold medal equestrian winner and international playboy. This brilliant Samurai warrior commanded the tough 26th Tank Regiment. He was a hard fighter right to the end and apparently left his fine boots behind.

We crawled forward past the boots, through an area of sparse, scraggly trees, kunai grass and craggy rocks. Another Marine, Emery Prine, and I inched to the right toward an opening between two gullies that converged into a "V." He took the right and I the left. A number of huge boulders, their insides carved out like pumpkins, lay on each side. These, of course, held snipers, and we had to keep low. I bellied forward losing sight of my companion in the heavily overcast day. Suddenly, it dawned on me that the deep bub-bub of American machine guns seemed more distant than the sharp tat-tat-tat of the Japanese guns. Artillery explosions seemed distant, too. I had gone too far. The signs showed that our men had been here but evidently fallen back.

Unable to determine which direction led back to our lines, lost amid identical looking rocks, I selected a random opening and wedged my way in. Every so often a peculiar-sounding "whoomp," impossible to identify as either friend or foe, waifed by. I noticed several helmets bobbing behind a large, house-sized rock, which appeared to be trying to conceal an old-fashioned gin-pole. It dawned on me that the helmets were Japanese and that they were servicing some type of weapon. The "whoomp" sound emanated from them. The gin-pole helped maneuver the heavy shells into firing position. I have since been told it was a huge spigot mortar, but it have been one of those wooden rocket launchers too.

Snaking along on my belly, the gully opened into a rocky, walled clearing strewn with wreckage and bodies. It offered little cover, but there was no other way to go. About halfway across, another movement caught my eye. A bobbing helmet approached from behind a sharp, jutting rock on the far side of the defile. I lay flat, belly down, on top of my Thompson, between two rotting Japanese bodies. I quickly skewed my helmet so the strap crossed my nose and covered one eye, then lay quiet.

Five Japanese, crouching, came into view, inching along a narrow path above me. They paused about 15-20 yards away and looked down at me. Each wore Marine dungarees, GI helmets and carried M-1 rifles. The last man in line wore regular Japanese trousers and leg wrappings. Pointing at me; they conversed. One picked up a baseball-sized rock and threw it hard against my back. Despite the sharp pain, my body lay motionless. Satisfied, they continued on in the direction from which I had come. The decaying gore cushioned me for at least another hour before my aching body crawled into a rocky niche.

Though safely concealed, I lay bone weary and scared. Did I sleep? I don't remember. Opening a ration called "tropical cheese" which had absorbed the odor of the two dead men who sandwiched me, I gagged. Everything had absorbed the stench. It was overpowering, more so than anything I had experienced on Saipan. There, bodies decomposed rapidly under the hot sun, and the odor quickly dispersed. But here the dankness, which had so disoriented me, seemed to radiate the putridness from every direction. Despite the cold and fog, sweat poured from my body. Then, it occurred to me that this area was nothing but a giant volcanic frying pan!

Iwo's hot volcanic ground was not only making me extremely uncomfortable but was slowly cooking the flesh of my mangled companions.

If it's stupid, but works, it ain't stupid

No doubt there were plenty of the enemy around, but they must have been occupied with more important matters than looking for a stupid Marine stumbling around this far behind the lines. Not giving a damn, I bolted out, vaulting over the two bodies, over rocks and other debris. In my panic, confusion reigned.

Gunfire reverberated, but was so distorted it could have come from any direction. Any direction I moved was a gamble. I eventually reached a walled, concrete ramp leading to the mouth of a large cave some 30 feet below. It resembled an entrance to a modern underground parking lot.

Obviously, I had stumbled upon an important enemy installation, possibly some type of headquarters or supply center.

A crenelated wall curved over the top of the cave where a sentry stood guard. He half sat, leaning forward, staring over the wall, his rifle beside him. Cautiously, I watched and waited for about half an hour, listening to distant gunfire. No movement in or out of the emplacement disturbed us. It puzzled me; there should be something going on, but the well-trained sentry remained focused. He peered intently toward a canyon that must have been an approach. Obviously, that was the direction from which the Marines would be coming and the direction I had to go. I would have to eliminate the sentry.

Crawling in a wide half circle to avoid the cave and the Japs inside, I tried to keep an eye on the man's back. I snuck within five feet of him, leaped up, cupped my hand over his mouth and shoved my K-bar (fighting knife) deep below his third rib, midway between his shoulder blade and spine. It was a perfect kill. Oh-oh, something didn't add up right.

Dragging the body aside, it appeared I had just killed an *already dead man.* How he died remains a mystery; concussion probably. His body bore no telltale mark, but he was stiff. I felt about as dumb as they come. I had wasted at least forty-five minutes stalking a corpse, when I could have just walked up, thumbed my nose and proceeded on.

A search of his pockets revealed only a tiny, three-tined brass pickle fork, which I tucked away. I worked my way down the cannon to our lines. Farther than anticipated, our Marines had fallen back somewhat. Looking down from a bluff, I spotted a wonderful sight; our guys with a couple of tanks. Hollering like hell, hoping they wouldn't shoot me, my butt slid down the embankment,. One of them greeted me with a cigar. I reported the gun position to a rocket battalion but couldn't really pin-point it on the map. I don't know if they knocked it out or not.

The following day, back with my crew, we came upon another cave. A ramp of loose shale marked the entry. Who would go first? I volunteered and crawled up, worming my way in, armed with my Thomson. A small crag in the stone lit the inside, most of the opening invisible from outside, yet it gave a wide view of the landing beach. A bloated dead man lay on a table. Crawling past another room filled with radio equipment, desks, etc, I hit the jackpot for trading material. Near one wall lay a tatami mat. Mindful of booby traps, I inched toward it. It looked way too inviting but never-the-less I lifted a corner to peek. Holy Mackerel! Six leather flap holsters, each containing a Smith & Wesson 44 caliber pistol[3] beckoned me. Trading material DELUX. Scrambling outside, I shared with my buddies--one for everyone and two for me.

---

[3]

The weapons had been sold to Japan in 1903. the snake brass buckle belts and ammo cases were of a type used in the Napoleonic wars and by the confederates in the American Civil War.

Chapter 31: If you are short of everything except the enemy, you are in combat

Laying in rotten guts is one of the few things that would force your buddies to deny you access to the ship. Upon returning, I stripped and threw my stinking dungarees in the boiling shell hole. The pool of hot water was good for washing clothes and heating food. The first time we washed clothing in it we hung the stuff to dry on one of the ship's cables. The Japanese mortar men took great offense to our laundry flapping in the breeze on one of their ships and hammered us with a barrage of mortar rounds and a couple of rockets, one of which did not explode. We never used that clothesline again.

Stark naked, I dove in another pool of refreshing, cold water trapped between our wreck and the ship sitting across from ours. The salt water felt good. Flopping around, I scrubbed off dirt and smell, and finally, much refreshed, hopped out. It had been a week or ten days since my boots had last come off. As I finger dried between my toes, a big ass shell exploded maybe 20 yards away. Scrambling for non-existent cover my nakedness felt more naked than ever! The shot had to be a stray, though. The Japs wouldn't waste a shell on me alone, and I certainly hadn't hung up any laundry!

Blood spurted from my foot. A piece of shrapnel had sliced neatly across the bottom of my arch, slick as a *razor*. I washed and dressed the cut and thought no more of it. Two or three days later, I discovered a bright red line running up from my ankle. Fortunately, a corpsmen handed me some sulfa tablets and told me to take one every four hours. I did not succumb to blood poisoning.

Good and bad news trickled in. We now held about half the island. Roads had been carved from the beach and over the terraces. Wreckage had been dynamited to clear the way for the landing craft, and a shit load of other wreckage had been sucked down into the black sands. What the black sands didn't claim the black surf did. Heavy shellings of the *LSTs* and *LSMs* lessened and focused on our front lines.

[*Roads had been carved from the beach*]

Even in our troop loses, good and bad news trickled in. Engel Bergsied's parents in Minnesota had been notified of his death, but in true twin fashion, his twin brother John, swore it wasn't true. He searched everywhere and questioned everyone until he found his brother alive, unconscious, on a hospital ship.

Lt. Paul Sumner and his crew, except for Frank, were dead. Aaron Riddle, a very good friend, went down with his tractor when rammed by an *LST*. Aaron, from Chicago, wanted only to go back, get his wife and kids and move to southern California. Several times, he told me he wouldn't make it through this campaign. I poo-pooed the statement.

If you are short of everything except the enemy, you are in combat

The case of the hijacked 10-in1 rations

An *LST* nosed into the beach directly in front of where Capt. Dan Reagan and his men were holed up. The vessel's captain called to Dan and asked if a work party could unload cases of 10-in-l rations, *asap*. He worried about mortar fire.

These, as opposed to Ks and Cs, were the caviar of combat rations. Each case held enough food for ten men for one day and contained a variety of canned meats, dried vegetables, bacon, fruit bars, dessert, cigarettes and, last but not least, toilet paper. Reagan immediately agreed to this unexpected bonanza and rounded up a work party. Everyone pitched in, including Baldy and Dan, who foresightedly donned enlisted men's jackets. The rapidity with which the ship emptied pleased the captain until he noted that the cases were not going to the assigned Air Force dump on the terrace. The Marines, racing from the ship, disappeared over a hill in the opposite direction.

A raucous blast from the ship's siren interrupted the hijacking, followed by a frantic command over the loudspeaker, "Hey, you men, you Marines, halt immediately! Come back here, that's an order!" The MPs swooped down. The last to emerge from the cavernous maw of the now-empty vessel was Eagan. He lugged out the very last case.

The ship's captain and an Army major responsible for the rations and livid with rage, complained loudly to the Shore Party commander, who then ordered the commanding officer of the 5th Amph Tracs, to report immediately and answer for this outrage.

Bill Stoll, always a master in such situations, took off the enlisted man's jacket and replaced it with his officer's jacket. He donned his most innocent expression and stepped out to face the music. Not recognized as a member of the work party, Bill played it to the hilt, acting surprised and shocked that PFC Eagan, one of *his* men, should be apprehended stealing rations.

"But," he protested, "this is too much of a hullabaloo over *one* man and *one* box of rations."

"One box!" screamed the flustered major. *"If* it were a matter of one god damned box, we wouldn't be here. An hour ago there were 1500 boxes on this god damned boat!"

"This is not a boat," countered the offended captain.

"I don't give a damn if it's Noah's Ark. I want my 1500 cases of rations."

"Well, Major," soothed Stoll, "it's obvious one person couldn't have taken that amount. However, leave it to me. I'll take this man into custody and will investigate."

The following morning they alerted Major Shead. He demanded an explanation. In spite of the smell of frying bacon wafting from foxholes throughout the entire area, no one knew a thing. The military police were so mad they grabbed one of our drivers, Louie Flores.

The bastards decided to interrogate Louie as a Japanese infiltrator in an American uniform! He had a slight build and ruddy complexion and they decided that was good enough for them. They dismissed his pleadings and were it not for Captain Stoll somehow taking custody of Louie back, he might have been shot.

Fortunately Louie did not give up the stash of beer and liquor that Stan Gienko and his crew had hidden under an overturned *LCVP*. The army major and MPs never did find it.

Food, whenever and wherever found, was always a blessing and, on at least one occasion, a real treat. Several of us on patrol stumbled upon a huge supply cave filled with hundreds of black rubber bags of rice and many tins of canned crab. Adjoining this cave was another loaded with, of all things, baseball bats, black Navy type oxfords and racks of torpedo heads. The oxfords, naturally, were all too small for me.

If you are short of everything except the enemy, you are in combat

Treasure of canned crab

Iwo was no doubt a well-stocked supply base that could have caused far more trouble had we not captured it when we did. At any rate, we were in no hurry to leave the confines of this cave and its treasure of canned crab. It could have been poisoned, but, like the tomatoes, what the hell.

It was delightful. It was superb. It was excellent. We stuffed ourselves and stayed longer than we should have. Darkness fell. For dinner, we had crab meat. It was, well, it was good, sort of. Toward morning we had the damned stuff for breakfast. We could barely gag it down. Time to leave.

On another occasion from the bowels of our "yacht," I climbed out of my sleeping quarters and began brewing coffee. The aroma acted as a magnet. Diditch, Cummings, Frenchy Naquin and others shuffled over. Lt. Malcolm started over from the officers' area, known as Ulcer Gulch, about a hundred yards away.

The Japanese still resented our using one of their naval craft, wrecked or not. It seemed to be a particular sore spot with them, and, when not occupied with other duties, they lobbed over mortars or rockets. This morning, however, they changed strategy and sprayed us with a light machine gun. Aboard ship, we were comparatively safe behind the ship's plating, but the strafing caught Malcolm out in the open. We hollered and signaled him to duck, but he plodded doggedly on in his big-footed, Colorado way. He strolled the entire distance unruffled and unscathed and climbed aboard, asking what in the hell we were yelling about. That Jap machine gunner must have been the most myopic individual in the entire Imperial Army!

We drank our coffee. Spike mentioned he had another assignment and told me to report to a captain waiting on the far side of the airfield, near a fork in the north trail that was now sort of a road. I grabbed my Thompson, some toilet paper, a canteen and K ration and headed out. I never carried a pack.

A scout and an infiltrator

The captain sat behind a field desk in a sheltered area that had been used as a forward field hospital. Field hospitals move with the front lines, remaining maybe only fifty yards to the rear. I recognized the location, because I had been treated there only last week. Plasma bottles, torn clothing, discarded helmets and weapons littered the area. We lost over 600 corpsmen and some 30 doctors on Iwo. I never did know for sure what happened to my Tobacco Doc. I knew him for only a few hours, but he was a great guy. My God, that was only two weeks ago.

Lt. Long made it all right. He had been all over the beach, never once thinking of his own safety. He did an excellent job of coordinating evacuation and saved hundreds of lives.

Paper work lay strewn on the field desk with a telephone in its midst. There were some non-coms handling other details. I gathered that this was a Grave Registration Team. This location wasn't really close to the front line. Confused, I thought it the wrong location. Reporting to the officer, I explained I was a scout and an infiltrator (a designation I had given myself) and that I knew nothing about grave registration. "What do you need me for?"

"Marshall, I need a man to help retrieve fallen Marines from the back areas off the trails " he said. The officer leaned forward rustling the papers on the desk, "You may not be familiar with our grave registry, but as an infiltrator, you know the area whereas my men don't. Lt. Malcolm assured me he'd send up the perfect man for the detail." Not sure it was a compliment, I wasn't particularly happy about this assignment.

Never-the-less if I was the best man for the job I *would do* the best job! I fashioned a hook from a ten-foot tent pole with a metal spike attached to the end. A nearby tank crew put aside repairing the vehicle's track long enough to bend the heavy spike for me. Armed with this elongated gaff, I hitched a ride on a recon vehicle by laying belly down on the wide fender, the pole out in front in the manner of a knight's lance. The road had been widened, allowing the trucks in the center, while replacement crews heading for the front trudged along each side.

We approached the area in question. Yes, it was familiar territory. My gruesome task began. For some reason, it never dawned on me that I had no crew. Maybe the officer didn't assign me a helper because I'd bragged about being a scout and an infiltrator.

The Japanese booby-trapped everything, their own dead included. I kept low and well back, stretched out the pole and hooked each body, carefully dragging it about five feet to determine if it were safe.

I laid the Marines' bodies on ponchos and pulled them back to the road. A sad job, I laid them out as neatly as possible, away from passing tanks and trucks. Enemy bodies were kicked over a cliff or thrown into the nearest hole or ditch. It took hours of creeping and crawling, but, eventually, I cleared the area in question. The captain thanked me and had another crew take over.

A shout from a nearby gully caught my attention. Even though tired, I trudged over to the caller. He may have known who I was but I didn't recognize him.

"Take a look at this," he indicated a group of men near the entrance of a cave. Their clothing did not look familiar compared to all the rest of us combat dirty Marines. "Naval Intelligence," my unknown friend informed me. I noticed the group were photographing what, looked to me, like a pile of garbage lying on the ground.

"Know him?"

I looked closer. Good God, a Marine, or what was left of him. I shook my head negatively. Even if I had known him, he was not recognizable. No ears, eyes gouged out, nose gone. What appeared to be his penis was shoved in his mouth. Large portions of skin had been peeled from his back and chest. What was left of the swollen face indicated he had been alive when these barbaric cruelties were inflicted. I felt guilty about my first impression of garbage. *My God, this man was a Marine.*

"We think his name was Iggy something, disappeared out of his hole a few nights ago, was just found this morning." Intelligence snapped more photos. I trudged away.

Exhausted and again filthy, I returned to my unit. The next day I asked the lieutenant why he laid that assignment on me. He scowled and said, "You were gettin' a little too smart-assed and careless. You needed some sittin' on. Any more questions?"

The lesson was a good one. I guess Reece and Spike did me a favor. I think maybe Stoll had something to do with it, too.

In the mean time, everyone had a job to do. Our armorers, Bob Phillips, Dick Austin, Auri Colmer, Walt Pechack, Walt Widak and some others, got a dozer and gouged a large trench in some of the more solid ground. They upturned one of our wrecked tractors over the trench, giving them a good solid armored roof. Inside, they set up lights and work benches and went to work rebuilding and repairing small arms brought back from the front. As soon as the weapons worked again, they raced them back to the front. Those guys worked night and day and put out a lot of rebuilt weapons from 30- and 50-caliber machine guns to carbines, Thompsons, Garands and even .45s. They deserve a lot of credit for the amount of work performed under very trying conditions.

Chapter 32: All five-second grenade fuses are really three seconds

It was another overcast day. Shuflata, Harbison, Rudd, Hugh Cummings, Billy Postel, Eagan, John Thomas and I cleaned out bypassed caves around Minami, an area above our beach position. Caves that could not be blasted shut had to be examined individually and neutralized.

Near a small amphitheater, we found a well-concealed cave. It was my turn to go in. Some rubble partially blocked the wooden door. At the bottom of a passageway carved in solid rock it was accessible by about ten or fifteen stone steps.

I forced open the heavy wooden door to allow passage and waited for my eyes to adjust in the gloomy interior. Pistol in hand—my Thompson remained back at the ship for some unknown reason. I edged further into the tunnel. Yardstick mines nestled in the junk on the floor. A body lay to my left at the entrance to a small connecting tunnel. In the dim light, I barely made out a bandaged, bare foot. Did my eyes deceive me or did that foot quiver?

At that same moment I sensed, or heard, a movement to my right. I crouched. The bare footed man attempted to jump up. I fired. The .45 slug caught him in the head. At the same time, a figure shouted and leaped from the dark. CLANK came the sound of metal on stone; a sword swung by my attacker. The blow aimed at my shoulder level hit the cave's stone wall before me.

The impact tumbled the soldier off balance and into me. Blindly, I locked my arm about his neck and shoulder, his face pressed against the side of my head. I buried the Colt .45 in his chest and fired again and again. He screamed something in my ear as the clip emptied. He slid from my grasp; his blood trailed down my dungarees. I nearly cut him in half.

A bone chip or slug scraped my left forearm and passed thorough his body, but I didn't know it until later, when I examined my torn and bloody sleeve. Each pistol flash illuminated my surroundings revealing another tunnel leading from the two I was in. Movement flickered from them, too, but further back. This was too much for me; Hubert Cummings threw another pistol to me from the entry, and I fired into the newly discovered opening and backed out.

Squeezing past the wooden door, I hollered for grenades. Johnny Shuflata threw me a white phosphorus grenade. With a pull of the pin and a hefty heave, a second later it came flying back out and rolled between my feet. I flew up the stairs, Cummings just ahead of me. The grenade went off, its burning white phosphorus singeing the back of my dungaree jacket.

Again instinctively, my feet brought me back down while I yelled for more grenades. Eagan threw one down but, without thinking, pulled the pin first. I relayed it into the cave just in time. It probably finished those remaining, but a Jap mortar crew spotted the brilliant white smoke from the phosphorus. They were very accurate in dropping shells so we beat it out of there. That ended our patrol for the day.

That night, sleeping in the bowels of the wreck, I awoke with a bad case of the shakes and a cold sweat. Visions of that sword coming at me invaded my sleep. I liked to draw and tried to make a sketch of the event but couldn't get my shaking hands to cooperate. It took a canteen cup of 100-proof medicinal alcohol, cut with grapefruit juice, and a half pack of cigarettes, for me to get back to sleep.

The next day I asked Eagan why he pulled the pin on the grenade he lobbed to me. "Oh, I just wanted to see if you were alert."

Not funny!

All five-second grenade fuses are really three seconds

Everyone took a beating on that island. Looking at my sketches now makes each event seem like it happened yesterday.

During a scramble near a concrete bunker, I somehow lost my .45 automatic just before a demo man threw a satchel charge through the gun port. The terrific concussion forced a Japanese officer into the open. He waved a pistol. Stunned and terribly confused, he staggered blindly about until shot by one of our men. I took his pistol and holster to replace mine and later headed back toward the beach with Hal Lewis, a tractor man who hailed from Wisconsin.

We took a narrow, winding trail from the north down toward the East Boat Basin. On the rocky beach we headed southward carefully, picking our way over and around boulders, ever on the lookout for infiltrators. Eventually, we came upon the engine room of a wrecked Japanese landing barge. It was not too far from where Pete Zarris and I had our adventure with the snipers in the cargo ship. This, too, merited investigation.

"Come out, come out, I won't shoot!"

Strolling up, I peered in. There were Japanese soldiers inside. They were as startled a I. I jumped back and yelled to Hal. We both ran for cover. One of the Japanese peeked around the edge of the hatchway.

I called out, *"Da tai koy, day tai koy, nua yu karo utsooso!"* meaning, or so I was told, "Come out, come out, I won't shoot!"

The man poked his head out a little further, smiled, and said, *"Hi, hi,"* meaning, "Yes, yes."

Lewis, a bit more suspicious, kept his pistol at the ready. For some reason, I decided to demonstrate a sense of fair play. Why, I don't know; perhaps I was tired of killing. I honestly thought we could take both Japs prisoner. My Japanese probably wasn't that good. I may have even called them a bad name or something. I laid my Japanese pistol on a small boulder in front of me and repeated that I wouldn't shoot.

One Japanese peered out. He kept nodding, smiling and repeating, *"Hi, hi,"* and began to slowly climb from the wreck, hands up.

He kept "Hi-hi"-ing. Then, I spotted a grenade cupped in his upraised hand. Scrambling for my pistol, he popped the cap against the metal overhead of the hatch. I snapped off a shot. Lewis fired at about the same time; one of us hit him in the throwing arm. Funny part of it was, until that moment I didn't even know if my weapon was loaded.

Gratefully, the grenade fell short. It exploded and I tumbled. My helmet flew off and I landed in rocks. Shaking the cobwebs from my brain, I heard Lewis fire several times.

Body parts? I took inventory. My left hand was a mass of blood. My ring finger was missing at the second joint. That made me mad. With a roar, I jumped up and charged. I could see the heads and shoulders of both men and fired at them from a distance of about four feet.

The weapon emptied yet my finger kept pulling the trigger. At the same time, two explosions filled the engine room with smoke. The steel bulkhead kept me from getting hurt again, but the acrid smoke blossomed into my face. When it cleared, the bodies of both men lay strewn, torn to pieces.

Damn. Killing us both was a real possibility for them. They had me down and dazed and with a little effort could have taken out Lewis on a two-to-one basis. Instead, they abandoned all, not only choosing death, but disobeying specific orders of their commanding officer, General Tadamichi Kuribayashi, and all that he stood for.

On closer examination of my finger stump, a piece of grenade shrapnel lay embedded in the knuckle. Turning my hand over, there lay my missing finger, bent, tightly crooked in my palm but still intact. My hand must have been clenched when I went down. The metal wedged in the joint prevented it from straightening out. I had more metal in my face and a sizable chunk in my shin. Lewis picked the stuff from my face, and I was able to pry the piece form the shin. We bandaged my leg, but the shard in the knuckle remained wedged tight. We made it back to our area where I found a mechanic (or a corpsman, I don't remember which) with pliers to remove the offending piece.

I did not know it at the time, but those two kills would be my last.

A few days later, while lying in my cubby hole on the ship, Johnny Shuflata and three or four others came aboard to see me. They had gone to the cave where I had my little adventure. Inside, they found four bodies, picked up some trophies: a couple of pistols and, best of all, the sword that kept me awake at night. They pointed out the nicks in the blade that were made when it had struck the cave wall.

A day or two later, I was back at the front line near Turkey Knob. A Japanese soldier rose from a hole, armed only with a piece of reinforcing rod sharpened into a spear. He charged a .30 machine gun which cut him in half.

Bone tired, I reached the command post overlooking a long gully. There were several officers and three or four Marines on radios and telephones. "Where should I go?" I asked amid the continuing onslaught of heavy gunfire in the gully. No one answered; they were all too busy to worry about another dumb replacement. I found a hole and lay back mentally blocking out sounds of mortar and small arms exploding above.

A guy jumped in alongside me. We shared a cigarette. He mentioned that he had seen a bird the day before. I didn't believe him. There were only flies and Japs on the island. "You're crazy. There are *no* birds!" He insisted he saw one.

"No way!" I blurted out. "No goddamned birds!"

I crawled out of the hole to the top of a small knoll. I turned my back on the gully. I was disgusted; that guy was crazy; no birds could live here; there were just no goddamned birds. That was that!

An officer, who must have been just off the ship, freshly shaved, wearing a shiny helmet and dressed in a clean uniform, raced up and began swearing at me.

Some of the words registered, "What the hell do you think you are doing sitting down . . . God damned slacker . . . sitting down . . . I'll show you some action . . . I'll put you down in that gully in the front lines where you belong!"

Sergeant Milks or Stoney Gragg, I don't remember who, came forward and apologized on my behalf to the officer. My rescuer then pulled me down behind a rock and handed me his whiskey-filled canteen.

The booze felt good. Bone weary, together we worked our way back to our command on Blue 2 beach.

Of more than a hundred tractors prior to Iwo, we now had only nineteen operable. It was obvious we would never make the *big* island of Okinawa as originally planned.

Strike on the merchant ship

A few days later, our squad was sent out to a merchant ship named *Hercules*— at least, I think that was the name. We were told by the ship's purser to get to work loading salvaged war material from a barge tied up alongside. "Why can't the merchant seamen do it," I grumbled and added that they looked healthier than us.

We were genuinely surprised at the answer.

They were on strike!

Their $300 bonus for being in a combat zone had not yet been approved! "You know, there has not been an air raid since

D + 2 more than a month ago, and, if you are worried about a combat zone, go ashore and see what one really looks like!"

Sitting on the hatch, I refused to move and dared any one of them to try and make me. We all felt the same. We were dirty, tired, bloody and not in a good mood. None of us moved. About an hour went by; it was pretty tense. After awhile one of the ship's officers came down and told us to get back in the *LCVP* that had ferried us out to this ship. We left.

Alligator Marines

[*One man always stays awake*]

Chapter 33: Leaving the Japanese Alamo

A couple of days later we boarded the *President Polk* and made for Hawaii. The *President Polk* had been a peacetime luxury liner and still retained the upper decks in that mode. The ship's officers and crew berthed there. The lower half of the ship, from the weather deck down, had been converted to the usual crowded, steamy, troop ship accommodations with no ventilation.

Fatigued, my battered body leaned against the rail as Iwo Jima, that battered rock, faded into the distance ... it looked so small. It was hard to believe so much occurred there and that the Japanese had fought so tenaciously to retain it. I couldn't help but compare that doomed garrison with the brave men who fought and died at that battered and worthless piece of American real estate known as the Alamo.

We were leaving all right, but a lot of our friends stayed.

Our first stop was Apra Harbor, Guam. Upon entering, orders came blaring over the ship's loudspeaker, "There will be no slovenliness." The captain of the President Polk orders, "all troops to bathe, shave, and get into clean clothing. Every man aboard has to look presentable while in harbor. Failure to comply will be a disobedience of orders and the miscreant will be confined below."

The hooting and ha ha's could be heard all over the harbor.

Only a sea bag full of war trophies accompanied me but no clean clothes. A salt-water shower with greasy soap was not at all inviting. Metal clamps held together a four-inch gash in my jaw. Ragged bloodstained bandages covered my left hand and right shin. The ripped out seat of my dungarees allowed my bare butt to flap in the breeze. One of my boots stunk to high heaven from stepping through a rotting Jap's belly.

All the other men were in similar condition. Our sentiments toward the captain of that ship were the same as when aboard the *Hercules* . . .he could stick it in his ear!

Late that night, I snuck into one of the several galley storage rooms. I pried a lock on a freezer and took as many two-gallon ice cream containers as would fit in my arms. They thumped and bumped, rolling down the steps of a gangway as an offering to the troops below. That would show that brass-hatted son-of-a-bitch! After all, there was a war on!

It was as if some of the brass didn't get it. Some did, like the unknown Marine with an ionic sense of humor. With all that had transpired in the prior month one thing had much impressed me. On my day of burial detail, I came across this message carved in soft volcanic rock:

> HERE LIE THREE DEAD JAPS
>   HEAR NO IWO
>   SEE NO IWO
>   SPEAK NO IWO
>   BY JIMA!

Chapter 34: The great adventure ends

We came ashore at Wailuku, Maui, grandly cheered by a huge crowd. "Welcome, Iwo Heroes," the banners read. We formed ranks as best we could. It was the only time 5th Amphs ever marched as a unit, and march we did ... no seat in my pants ... down the main street to waiting trucks.

The people of Maui were wonderful. They hugged us, they cheered and they cried. They handed us flowers, dainties and even beer. It felt as though I made *real Marine*. We had no idea we were heroes of Iwo Jima. We were unaware of the overall carnage that had maimed our ranks, and we knew nothing of the flag-raising photograph taken by Joe Rosenthal or the motion pictures by Sgt. Bill Genaust. Nor did we know President Roosevelt proposed a special medal be struck for us.

[*I knew Sergeant Bill Genaust, military photographer, from Saipan and when he spotted me and Eagan, he asked us to hold still for a photo. We semi-posed by a sentry box with Mt. Suribachi in the background. We heard that a few days later he*

was killed by a Japanese squad. If they ever recover his body, and time hasn't destroyed the film, they may find this picture in his film pack.]

Mail call was first on the agenda. How in the world had mail caught up with us? Everyone spent hours reading and rereading every precious sentence. They handed me a few notes from my parents plus a bonus, a letter from the beautiful Theresa!

Clean dungarees and a fresh-water shower—boy, what a treat! Shaving was difficult because of the metal clamps in my chin. However, it didn't matter, as we were allowed a week of leisure before starting training in brand new *LVT-3* amphtracs.

It was time to catch up on many of my rough sketches. Eagan asked why I wasted time on sketching when we had beer to drink.

"Some day, I'll put them in a book."

"What the hell for?" he growled. "Nobody will believe 'em anyway." His enthusiasm was overwhelming.

Our new quarters were tents on well-laid-out streets. Showers had been built, as were the heads which had walls around them! Old habits die hard, though, and, when a work party was assigned clean-up detail, someone tossed a pint of gasoline down the hole. Before moving the wooden structure. A spectacular blaze ensued.

They provided us with a movie house and we didn't even have to come armed. Best of all was the beer garden. The guys attempted to drink it dry every night but never succeeded. The only sad note, besides the loss of our buddies, was our faithful companion, Samson. He did too good a job guarding our area and bit a paperboy. The law required that he be disposed of. It was done honorably. He refused a blindfold.

Liberty was allowed on a regular basis. The towns of Wailuku and Lahaina were not far away, and we always had a good time. My first liberty in Lahaina was a doozy. I got very drunk and wound up in an ancient stone dungeon some place in the center of town. Everyone remained tolerant, though. One wrinkled and grandmotherly lady recognized me from the parade on the day we arrived. This grandmother told me how sorry she felt for us and how tired and ragged we looked marching through Wailuku. To my embarrassment, she mentioned the lack of a seat in my pants.

The new tractors were really something, twin Cadillac engines with hydromatic transmissions, a luxurious driver compartment and plenty of room in the cargo area. Boy, these were the babies we would drive right into the land of the Rising Sun.

We had a small ceremony for awards. Someone said I might get a Silver Star for repeated exposure to enemy fire while carrying ammo up and wounded back, but that went by the board. My Purple Heart was denied because there was no record of my wounds or treatment. Christ, the final tally on Iwo was the loss of 627 corpsmen and 23 doctors--with untold wounded. Who did they expect to keep records under those conditions? I didn't make an issue of it.

Our rigorous training continued. We honed our skills, studied our mistakes and prepared for the really big one, *Japan* itself.

We heard of a bomb so big it wiped out a whole city

Then, one day, we heard of a bomb being dropped, a bomb so big it wiped out a whole city. Naturally, I didn't believe it and smugly pointed out the largest airplane in the world couldn't carry a bomb that damn big.

A few days later we heard of another bomb and another city. The same thing. I stuck to my guns. We were in the theater later in the week getting instructions on a Shoepack; a large canvas tote bag containing everything we would need for the cold, snowy weather in Japan.

While the instructor spoke, a message was handed him. He walked to the wings of the stage, then came back and said, "I don't know about you guys, but I'm going home. *The war is over.*"

Homeward bound

Almost everyone cheered, but Eagan and I didn't. That bomb meant there would be no invasion. We felt we hadn't killed enough enemy. There were others who felt the same. Lt. Carl Lauer, with great foresight, wanted to go clear through to Japan and then start on the Russians.

We returned to the U.S. aboard the battleship Colorado. En route we hit a terrific storm; the old battle wagon bucked and plunged like a bronco for three days but no one cared. It was homeward bound!

At San Diego, pom-pom girls, a brass band, the Red Cross and the Salvation Army met us.

Before we debarked, the Salvation Army broadcast that they would be happy to send telegrams, free, to our families, if we would just write our names, the address desired, and hand the info to one of their people. We scribbled furiously, and most everyone enclosed a coin or bill with the message. We then tossed the weighted bundles to waiting hands on the dock below. They were good to their word, and hundreds of parents and sweethearts received the good news within a very short time. We had been gone about nineteen months. Some of the guys were surprised to find out they were brand-new papas.

On December 3, 1945, a group of us sat in a chapel at Camp Pendleton. A priest began lecturing, "Only you who hated the war have the right to be proud. Only you who did not wish to go should be given the credit. Only you who left your job and family have a claim to the honor of accomplishment in this great victory ..."

The great adventure ends

I sat there stunned. What the hell was this jackass talking about? True, I didn't give up as much as some of the fellows, but there were many more like me, and some of us bled and lay weeks with crushing fevers; some of use gave arms and legs, and some gave their lives.

He blabbed on and on, finally winding up with, ". . . Only those of you that I have outlined deserve the credit and blessings of God." Yeah, thanks.

The fool must have thought the rest of us were on vacation. Looking forward, not back, Eagan and I later received our separation pay. Mine was corporal's pay of $66 per month, which accumulated, amounted to $156.18 plus $4.35 for travel expense.

Someone handed me two manila envelopes. One contained my honorable discharge and DD-214. The other contained a mimeographed paper that began, "Corporal Donald B. Marshall, #548790USMCR," and went on, "... hand grenade shrapnel wounds to the left hand are acknowledged. However, because the wounds do not meet the 20% disability criteria, disability benefits are denied."

I hadn't asked for any benefits and hadn't reported any wounds. Then it occurred to me. At least one of those front-line corpsmen who treated me was not killed, and somehow the record of my treatment had just now caught up.

Oh, well ... I still didn't get a Purple Heart.

Eagan and I shouldered our sea bags, walked out of Pendleton's main gate and stood alongside the Coast Highway. The bright California sun shone down. A car roared up the highway. We sort of hoped it was Danny Reagan driving that old *Pierce-Arrow*. It wasn't.

"Now what do we do?" asked my buddy.

I shrugged.

We stuck out our thumbs.

Chapter 35: Epilogue

I BECAME A MARINE

Leaving the Marine Corps in December of 1945, Eagan and I teamed up. We bummed around the country, worked in a coal mine in Utah, the Forestry Service in California and Clyde Beatty's circus through several other states. Finally I left him on a ranch in Utah and headed back to school and a diploma. Eventually, Eagan went back in the Corps.

I qualified for the Los Angeles Police Department. Training was just like boot camp. Hollywood Boulevard was my first beat. Nice, but no action. I transferred to San Pedro and walked the Beacon Street waterfront, the toughest beat on the coast.

The Korean War began. I volunteered for the Army requesting tank duty, citing my experience in the Corps. Much to my disgust, they assigned me to MP duty at Camp Roberts, California.

This war passed me by. When it ended, my job at the police department awaited me.

Assigned to downtown Los Angeles Central Division, one day Lieutenant Sam Posner called me to his office. Sam and a police inspector invited me to take a seat.

"Marshall," the lieutenant began, "we know you were a Marine in the Pacific, and we know what you went through. How do you feel about the Japanese today?"

"I don't feel one way or another. The war is six years behind. I did my job; they did theirs."

That scorching letter my dad had written to me on Saipan came to mind.

"Fine," said the inspector. "We have a problem. The Japanese are opening up businesses along First Street. There's been some local animosity, and they have asked for a beat

Epilogue

officer, one they could rely on. If you have no objections, we would like to give the assignment to you.

Always enjoying a beat assignment, I accepted.

The following day found me prepared for anything. I introduced myself to each proprietor on the small, neat shops along the beat and then to the priests at the Buddhist temple. I informed all that they would find me receptive to any problems they might encounter. My new beat received me warmly along the entire route.

A week went by without incident. One day a small Japanese gentlemen emerged from the Ginza, a basement restaurant on First Street.

"My name Jimmu. I own tis prace. You Mr. Marshaw?"

"I am."

"Ahhh, you Maline in Pacific?"

"I was."

"Ahhh, you biig man. You fight Japanese sodjer?"

A cloud of suspicion boiled up in my mind. They're all just too damned nice. Finally I would find out what they and this little bastard were planning.

"You shoot Japanese sodjer?" he continued.

"*Yes*," I snapped, alert for any sudden move.

"You get wounded?"

"*No!*" the lie spilled out; I wouldn't give him the satisfaction.

"Ooooh, you biig man." He spread his arms. "Biig target, you no get wounded. Hah, I write retter to emperor and tell him Japanese sodjer berry berry bad shot!"

Looking at this little Japanese man named Jimmu . . . all the suspicions built up inside vanished. I began to giggle. Jimmu's face was totally devoid of any expression except . . . total innocence. The more I looked at him, the harder I laughed.

207

Epilogue

He joined in. We locked arms and went below for a glass of Saki.

Ted Williams's words from so long ago went through my mind, "Some day, kid, you'll make a Marine."

This was that day.

[*Don Marshall, Los Angeles Police Detective*]